JUVENILE
DELINQUENCY
RESEARCH, THEORY AND COMMENT

Bernice Milburn Moore

Assistant to the Director
Community Services and Professional Education
The Hogg Foundation for Mental Health
The University of Texas

Consultant
Home and Family Education
Texas Education Agency
Austin, Texas

ASSOCIATION FOR SUPERVISION AND CURRICULUM DEVELOPMENT
A department of the National Education Association
1201 Sixteenth Street, N.W., Washington, D. C. 20036

Copyright 1958 by the
ASSOCIATION FOR SUPERVISION AND CURRICULUM DEVELOPMENT

A department of the National Education Association

1201 Sixteenth Street, N.W.

Washington, D.C. 20036

Price $1.00

Second Printing
August 1960

The Library of Congress has catalogued this
publication as follows:

Moore, Bernice Milburn
   Juvenile delinquency: research, theory and comment.
Washington, Association for Supervision and Curric-
ulum Development [1958]

   vii, 68 p. 23 cm.

   Bibliographical footnotes.

   1. Juvenile delinquency.

HV9069.M72   364.36   58-59835

Library of Congress

Contents

From the Association

MUCH HAS been said about juvenile delinquency. Opinions on causes and on how the problem should be handled are reported freely in newspapers and magazines. Most findings of research, however, seem to substantiate the judgments of scholars in the field, that delinquency is a problem of great complexity. Much useful and reliable information is available, but no over-all solutions are in sight. Although teachers are not expected to be experts in the field, it is a generally recognized fact that what schools do can make a difference in the prevention and control of delinquency. This booklet was prepared to help provide a reliable and useful source of information to help schools assume their role as wisely as possible in regard to the problem of juvenile delinquency.

The Association is especially grateful to Bernice Milburn Moore and to her co-workers for their careful and painstaking work in locating, examining and interpreting research studies and for reporting their findings in *Juvenile Delinquency: Research, Theory and Comment.* This booket will be useful to school personnel who are continually seeking better solutions to the problem of preventing and alleviating juvenile delinquency.

The Association is also indebted to members of Study Group 47 on Juvenile Delinquency of the Tenth Conference of ASCD for their contributions to the origin and preparation of some of the material.

William M. Alexander, professor of education, George Peabody College for Teachers, Nashville, Tennessee, served as reader for the Executive Committee. Rodney Tillman, executive secretary, ASCD, read the galleys and gave helpful editorial suggestions. Robert R. Leeper, editor and associate secretary, ASCD, edited the final manuscript and was in charge of its publication. Ruth P. Ely, editorial assistant, ASCD, guided technical production of the booklet and secured permissions to quote.

JANE FRANSETH, *President,*
September 1958   *For the Executive Committee*

v

Introduction

THIS BOOKLET on juvenile delinquency does not attempt a full review of the literature. Over the past ten years much has been written on this topic that is flamboyant in seeking popularity, while some of the writing is firm in its scientific sincerity. Realization is growing that delinquency is not only an intricate problem in itself but that research in this area is also multiphasic and difficult.

Presented here, therefore, is an indication of the popular approach, a discussion of difficulties in enumerating offenders, information which will be useful in distinguishing normal and healthy rowdiness and buoyancy from behavior pathology, a résumé of the best theories thus far advanced in the field, and a quick view of the schools' approach to the problem. The design has been to assist with an understanding and appreciation of the social-psychological problems of deviant behavior

Special appreciation is expressed to Harry Estill Moore, professor Department of Sociology, and to Robert L. Sutherland, director, The Hogg Foundation for Mental Health, both of The University of Texas for their help on content validity, in constructive and careful criticism of presentation, and in editing the manuscript. Since the materials used are broad in their behavioral and social science import, the counsel of these two persons was indispensable in preparation of the final document.

As will be apparent in the footnotes, a group of persons made substantial contributions to the origin and preparation of this discussion This was Study-Discussion Group 47 on Juvenile Delinquency at the Tenth Conference of the Association for Supervision and Curriculum Development, NEA. Letters from some of the participants in this group are quoted as well as materials later sent for consideration and use. To all who participated in the study-discussion group and to those whose letters and materials were used, an expression of gratitude is made.

Since this writing project has been under way some three years Robert R. Leeper, editor of publications for the Association for Super vision and Curriculum Development, deserves a heartfelt "thank you" for patience and encouragement. Through arrangement with the Association, Roy Eagles, now of London, England, was made available for bibliographical work and should be remembered for his early interest and help. Without Mary Beth Holmes Curtis, this document could not have been completed in its present form. She, too, gave valuable assistance with documentation. She has prepared the final manuscript and has taken care of numerous details involved in this work.

If what has been written proves helpful even to a few parents, teachers or school administrators, then the effort will be worth while.

July 1958   BERNICE MILBURN MOORE

CHAPTER 1

Juvenile Delinquency—
A Much Publicized Problem

HEADLINES in both large and small newspapers, over radio and television, and in all types of magazines shout about "juvenile delinquency." These references are frequent, often condemnatory and inflammatory, as they picture the misbehavior of today's children and youth in communities throughout the United States, as indeed in other nations of the world.

Perhaps no social problem in the current scene draws as much attention as juvenile delinquency and—as is true of so many other such intricate problems—no over-all solution is in sight. Delinquency among youth is a part of the dynamic process of social change even as are crime, divorce, alcoholism, race riots, and other attempts at adjustment through maladjustment.

World War I and World War II both noted an upswing in overt misbehavior among the young. Attempts were made to inhibit its development during these cataclysmic years through the schools, through youth centers and other community efforts, and by parents as well as law enforcement officers.

Delinquency in wartime is one thing, but a continuing rise in youth crime and delinquent behavior among children in peacetime is quite another. The present period of nationwide concern rose to its peak with the intensive work of the United States Senate's Judiciary Subcommittee to Investigate Juvenile Delinquency, which began its activities in 1953 under the chairmanship of Senator Estes Kefauver. Since then there has been little cessation of publicity on the problem, and it has risen to a crescendo with the recent New York City public school uproar and with the sex crimes and beatings, to say nothing of murders of the young by the young throughout the nation.

That juvenile delinquency is a cause for concern is true. That such

1

2

consistent and often flamboyant anxiety as expressed in the press and magazines is helpful, is highly questionable. Erik H. Erikson, noted psychiatrist and theorist in the fields of behavior and social-emotional development, finds within it real danger.

Dr. Erikson commented during a recent conference on research and delinquency:

. . . it seems that what is written about juvenile delinquency—even by well-meaning people—is one of the most malignant aspects of the phenomenon. . . .

. . . I think juveniles are especially aware of and sensitive to what is being said about them. They constantly look for, and develop by, the reflections of themselves in others. Therefore, when one publishes something about this subject, one must remember that juveniles will read it. One cannot write about them without writing for them. And if one reports nothing but adult bewilderment and self-contradiction, one represents the adult world as untrustworthy. So, in a way, one justifies juvenile delinquency. . . .[1]

Richard Clendenen, executive director, and Herbert W. Beaser, chief counsel, for the Kefauver Subcommittee distilled volumes of testimony into readable language and size for public consumption in their series of five articles in the *Saturday Evening Post* beginning on January 8, 1955. For those who work with children and youth, no better documentation of the problem in popular form can be found. These men wrote in their first article:

. . . we crisscrossed the United States repeatedly since November of 1953 to study conditions that have caused an amazing increase of 45 per cent in law infractions by youngsters in the last five years. . . . We have been aided by countless state and local officials worried by an unprecedented total of 1,000,000 kids who came into conflict with authority last year. We have been aided by many experts in the field who predict that the total will mount to more than 2,000,000 annually by 1960 unless drastic action is taken. . . .[2]

The conclusion of this study as reported by these men is that juvenile delinquency is everybody's business and specially that of teachers, parents and community personnel.

Agreement of the findings of this Subcommittee with the research of sociologists, criminologists, psychologists and psychiatrists is close. Both findings and research affirm that the problem is complex and

[1] Helen L. Witmer and Ruth Kotinsky, editors. *New Perspectives for Research on Juvenile Delinquency*. Children's Bureau Publication No. 356. Washington, D. C.: U. S. Department of Health, Education, and Welfare, 1956. p. 2-3.

[2] Richard Clendenen and Herbert W. Beaser. "The Shame of America." *Saturday Evening Post*, January 8, 1955. p. 17. See also issues for January 15, 22, 29, and February 5, 1955.

contradictory. Slums _do_ breed delinquency. Yet millions of sturdy citizens began their lives in families which lived in slums or under slum conditions. Rejection and overindulgence of children by parents have contributed to the growing list of offenses, but others suffering under the impact of these same experiences are not delinquents. Children and youth from "rich" homes as well as "poor," from the "right" neighborhoods and well as the "wrong," have gotten into trouble. Why some youngsters indulge in delinquent behavior, and others do not, is the "stickler" question. Without this contradiction, scientific theory and research would be infinitely simpler.

In an interview in _Newsweek_, September 17, 1954, Richard Clendenen of the Kefauver Subcommittee listed divorce, poverty, crime, comics, slums, and strong drink as contributing forces in the rise in delinquency rates. On the curative side, he suggested the strengthening of family life, better institutions for offenders, self-regulation of the mass media which reach children and youth, more careful parental control, and a fundamental love of children by parents, as steps in the right direction.

Interviews with judges and law enforcement officers, on conditions of youth crime in New York, Chicago, Philadelphia, Minneapolis and Milwaukee, took up 10 full pages of _Newsweek_, January 14, 1955.

Conclusions were reproduced in table form listing causes and cures of youth crime.[3] Some of the causes outlined were these: general disregard for constituted authority; weak discipline in homes and schools; leniency in juvenile courts; probation resulting in "too many repeaters"; few good institutions for juvenile offenders; shortage of trained probation personnel; "comic" books too vicious for children; and policemen untrained in handling youthful offenders.

As steps in the right direction, these officials offered: increase in parental respect for the law and teaching of such respect to their children; firmer control of children and youth by their parents; less "coddling" of young hoodlums; more severe treatment for "repeaters"; reformatories which will reform; control of comic books; and welltrained policemen to work with youngsters on neighborhood beats. No one will gainsay the validity of these procedures for improvement of youth behavior, but how they may be accomplished is something else again.

A recent article[4] attempts to simplify the whole matter by suggesting "Nine Words That Can Stop Juvenile Delinquency," these words being

[3] _Newsweek_, January 14, 1955. p. 67.
[4] _Reader's Digest_, March 1958. p. 106.

"Put Father back at the head of the family." This is in complete contrast to the report on the research of Fritz Redl described by Charles B. Seib and Alan L. Otten in an article in *Harper's*, January 1958, on "The Case of the Furious Children." [5]

Still another popular presentation of the problem has been written in a comprehensive series of articles under the title, "The Shook-Up Generation," by Harrison E. Salisbury, Pulitzer Prize winner, in *The New York Times*, from March 23 through 30, 1958. This informal survey will be quoted at some length in that the delinquency situation as it has shown itself in problems of behavior in the New York public schools has been widely publicized throughout the nation and the world. Salisbury attempts to write "a perceptive report on the juvenile gangs of New York—why they are formed, how they exist in a world they help to make, what might be done about them, what the city *is* doing."

Salisbury points out that the influence of gangs runs far wider than the gangs themselves and permeates the thinking and feelings of all youth. He remarks that gangs are "pitiful, tragic, dangerous" and that youth caught within them seek a way out which is hard, if not almost impossible, to achieve.

Gangs, Salisbury states, as others have stated before him, are products of social deterioration and are found in their very worst form in slum areas and areas of over-all social deprivation. He lists "defense and comradeship" as basic motivation for gang membership. Moreover, ethnic and racial problems alone are not at the root of gangs in New York. A general disintegration of social organization exists in large underprivileged areas where many ethnic and racial groups are intermixed.

Lack of basic security in families, in neighborhoods, in community life, Salisbury points up as fundamental to the trouble in the schools. The gang offers a dubious substitute for security which does not exist in the present and for which there is no promise in the future. For most gang members, he writes ". . . just to get through today and this week or this month is enough. Their perspective doesn't go any further." [6]

Turbulence among youth may be traced to families living below the subsistence level in crowded quarters and with little immediate promise of better situations. Moreover, Salisbury holds that there has been a real loss to New York, and to any city, by the movement out of its environs to suburbia of young and energetic persons in power

[5] Charles B. Seib and Alan L. Otten. "The Case of the Furious Children." *Harper's Magazine*, January 1958. p. 56-61.

[6] Harrison E. Salisbury. Reprint from *The New York Times*, March 23-30, 1958. p. 5. See complete report: Harrison E. Salisbury, *The Shook-Up Generation*, New York: Harper and Brothers, 1958.

positions capable of new and creative approaches to community problems.

Schools, Salisbury insists, are in most instances the only haven of security and refuge for the thousands of youngsters buffeted by poverty, family inadequacy, lack of informal and formal neighborhood organization, migration from one culture to another, and with no other positive outlet for their interests and energies. Many youth, if they are unfortunate enough to live in impoverished neighborhoods lacking resources for youth activities which are available to middle class areas, find their only stimulation and real opportunity for free association in groups at the school.

"Tools and techniques" for working out the problem of delinquency in New York—and in any other community—are available. While Salisbury indicates the cost would not be too high, others are of the opinion that the coordination and utilization of even available resources would be expensive in money but not overly costly in terms of value received. He stresses that problems of delinquency can be met only by unified effort, creative imagination, and above everything else, personal responsibility and concern on the part of powerful citizens in all groups within the city.

If it is any solace to the United States with its problems among youth, Salibury writes that the Soviet Union, with which he is familiar, faces the same, if not an even more severe, socially destructive situation. Other nations as well, he indicates, are in the throes of bringing into social usefulness a large number of potentially productive youngsters now delinquent in their activities.

Salisbury offers a warning to New York City readers which is applicable to persons throughout the nation. The number of juvenile delinquents is not overly large. As Salisbury describes the situation:

An enormous percentage of the 906,000 youngsters in the New York public schools are ordinary children, untouched by gang psychology. They are interested in their studies, enjoy an occasional skylark, but are a credit to their parents and the community. This goes for children of all races, colors and creeds.[7]

And it should be emphasized that this goes for children and youth in the United States as a whole, as later data will indicate.

Thus, popular writings run the gamut from the scare headlines, destructive in themselves on many fronts, to careful reports of tentative research in the behavior of the socially and psychologically maladjusted, such as the article concerning Redl's work and the journalistic survey of Harrison E. Salisbury.

[7] *Ibid.*, p. 8.

CHAPTER 2

Youthful Delinquents—
How Many? Do We Know?

HOW WIDESPREAD is delinquency in the United States? A direct answer to this question is not and cannot be known at present. This blank area of information arises from almost complete lack of uniformity in definitions of delinquent acts by different communities and even by different personalities involved in law enforcement within the same community.

The difficulties in obtaining accurate information on how many youth and children participate in delinquent behavior are summarized by Bloch and Flynn:

1. Lack of uniformity in reporting and no compulsory registration of youthful offenders;

2. Differences in the way courts classify and handle delinquents;

3. Variations in how youngsters with problems are referred to community agencies for handling;

4. Variations in the methods of reporting the reception of children in institutions; and

5. Differences in the way police handle and refer children for misbehavior.[1]

As has also been noted, families of middle and upper class children serve as buffers between their children and their inclusion among the delinquent population of the nation.

In a study on the measurement of the extent of juvenile delinquency, D. W. Wilson points out that there are two types of crime in which youth indulge: offenses known to police, and offenses less likely to be or become known to police, such as drunkenness, arson, fraud, and sex offenses.[2] The only figures available which are accurate are

[1] Herbert A. Bloch and Frank T. Flynn. *Delinquency: The Juvenile Offender in America Today.* New York: Random House, 1956. p. 25.

[2] D. W. Wilson. "How to Measure the Extent of Juvenile Delinquency." *Journal of Criminal Law and Criminology*, 42:435-38; 1951-52.

those reported on arrests, and this is a statement of arrests and not of offenses.

Not only do the above problems enter into determining the actual presence or absence of delinquency, but there is also wide discrepancy in definition of the terms "juvenile," "misbehavior," and "delinquency" from state statute to state statute. Sometimes these range from descriptions of adult misdemeanors and felonies through such highly subjective terminology as "incorrigibility" or "ungovernable behavior." [3]

There are, nevertheless, indicators of delinquency and its relative rise and fall. Schwartz makes an interesting comparison. He describes the similarity of trends between the Federal Bureau of Investigation's statistics of youth crime, obtained since 1930 from local and state police and published in its *Uniform Crime Reports*, and those of the Children's Bureau with its collected reports from juvenile courts since 1926.[4] While neither of these reports is complete for the nation nor accurate in terms of uniformity of definition, together they do point up a trend. As charted, these two sets of figures showed a peak in 1945 and a decided downswing in 1948. Since then there has been a steady upward trend.

In the most recent figures on youth crime released by the Federal Bureau of Investigation and published throughout the nation in the newspapers of April 23, 1958,[5] Director J. Edgar Hoover noted an upsurge in youth crime with an increase of some 55 percent since 1952 among persons under 18. However, Hoover makes a sharp distinction between juvenile crime, as reported in the statistics from his Bureau, and juvenile delinquency. If, as Schwartz points out, juvenile delinquency rates as gathered by the Children's Bureau, and those of juvenile crime brought together by the FBI, do run a parallel course, it seems safe to suggest that delinquency as well as crime among youth has had a sharp upswing in the past six years. How sharp the upswing has been in delinquency is much harder to determine than in crimes committed and arrests made.

Two conclusions are apparent. First, from every available evidence, statistical and nonstatistical, the problem of delinquent behavior is both intense and real. Second, whatever statistics are quoted to back a conservative or a radical or a middle-of-the-road position on the extent of delinquency must be quoted as *indices* and not as *facts*.

[3] Edward E. Schwartz. "Counting Delinquent Children." *Children*. November-December 1954, p. 227-31.

[4] *Ibid.*, p. 229-30.

[5] Associated Press release as published in the *Austin* (Texas) *Statesman*, April 23, 1958. p. 1 and 3.

CHAPTER 3

Behavior—Normal, Emotionally Disturbed, or Delinquent?

WITH THE IMPACT of publicity, it is little wonder that parents, teachers and other adults become perplexed concerning behavior of youngsters. Some findings from recent studies will be presented which make an attempt to distinguish between normal, healthy personalities, those suffering from emotional disturbances or character disorders, and those who are definitely delinquent. Teachers and school administrators will recognize helpful concepts in all of these findings. These concepts will be useful in recognizing behavior at school which may be handled as normal problems of normal youngsters; behavior which demands immediate therapy and treatment by clinicians; and behavior which is of such nature and origin that legal and social work agencies should be quickly involved in handling it. As has been pointed out succinctly by Bertram M. Beck,[1] too often teachers and school administrators have been expected to do something about everything! Some behavior, he notes, lies entirely outside the province and the competence of teachers.

The teacher's fundamental interest always lies in the educational achievement of children taught in groups. Children are sent to school to learn. If this is to be accomplished, social pressures demand that children conform to expected classroom behavior so that all may learn and share. Herein is the great difference in the relationship of the teacher to youngsters in the classroom where group controls of behavior have to operate efficiently, and the relationship of the child to the clinician in an office situation where "acting out" is permitted and expected as a part of treatment. More and more it is being recognized that achieving understanding of children's behavior is not a one-way street. Teachers have much to offer clinicians from their

[1] Bertram M. Beck. "The School and Delinquency Control." *Annals of the Academy of Political and Social Science*, November 1955. p. 60.

group experiences, even as clinicians have important knowledge which is useful to the teacher from his therapist-patient relationship.[2]

Healthy Defiance

Paul W. Tappan, criminologist, has called attention to the danger of equating normal, active behavior with prophecy of danger, as a sign of impending delinquency. He also stresses the confusion which exists between delinquent behavior and the behavior of the emotionally disturbed. He comments that authoritarian methods with the disturbed child who is not delinquent may well produce what it is desired to avoid.[3]

In a Chicago Round Table Discussion on the prevention of delinquency and maladjustment of youth on May 3, 1953, a group of experts from several fields of study reminded the audience that the normal, *healthy* aggressiveness of youth must not be confused with delinquency. Moreover, they called attention to the often overlooked fact that youth can and do change. Occasional slips in behavior which may be classified as delinquent in no way indicate youth will become confirmed delinquents.[4]

Misbehavior on occasion by children and youth should be as expected as it is among adults! In his study of pre-college and college youth, Austin Porterfield found that among 437 students, all admitted delinquent behavior in one way or another on one or more occasions. These young people included both men and women.[5]

Howard Lane states this even more imperatively in a mimeographed paper, entitled, "The Meaning of Disorder Among Youth":

"Teen-ager" has become the journalistic equal of "hoodlum, gangster, junior public enemy." This stereotype makes less sense than to attribute common characteristics to people in their thirties, or sixties. Knowing this in their bones numerous youth are resentfully playing roles assigned them. The fact of increased discontent and disorder among our near-adult population is clearly established. Thus far America's response to it is one of

[2] George A. W. Stouffer, Jr. "Behavior Problems of Children as Viewed by Teachers and Mental Hygienists: A Study of Present Attitudes as Compared with Those Reported by E. K. Wickman." *Mental Hygiene*, April 1952. p. 285.

[3] Paul W. Tappan. "Sociological Motivations of Delinquency." *American Journal of Psychiatry*, March 1952. p. 680-84.

[4] Paul Bowman, Frank Flynn, John Havighurst, Robert J. Moorman and C. Fabriola. "The Prevention of Delinquency and Emotional Maladjustment of Youth." *University of Chicago Round Table, Number 786*. Chicago, Illinois: University of Chicago. May 3, 1953.

[5] Austin Porterfield. *Youth in Trouble*. Austin, Texas: The Leo Potishman Foundation, 1946. p. 38-39.

anger, threatened reprisals, loud calls for more restriction, repression, punishment, and varieties of lolly-poppy youth programs. Current research and sober reflection show clearly that disorder and discontent have not been diminished by them. . . .[6]

Tappan agrees with Lane that the application of epithets or predictions of delinquency should be avoided in every conceivable instance in order to minimize the possibility of forcing normal youngsters into association with those who are true delinquents.[7] Bertram M. Beck goes even further and suggests that a form of "accidental delinquency" may occur when youth are forced to form their self-images as delinquent because adults in their lives, including teachers, are too inflexible in their definitions of normality.[8]

Robert Linder, a psychologist in Baltimore before his recent death, saw dire results of forced conformity in the increasingly violent behavior of youth. He believed that society, as expressed through education, social work, recreation, pediatrics, mental hygiene, philosophy and religion, demands that youth conform, submit and adjust. The answer to these pressures for conformity, Linder stated, is not only rebellion but downright hostile mutiny—or, as Beck indicates, accidental delinquency. Linder believed he had discovered, in the mutiny against conformity, the reason back of misbehavior on the part of normal youth and the explanation for the increasing brutality of youth crime. Obviously this situation cannot be placed solely at the feet of youth, but has been created by "the blunders, illusions, mistakes, and misconceptions" of the adults who have fallen for the philosophy of conformity.[9]

A far less dramatic approach to youth behavior is taken by Fritz Redl, chief, Laboratory for Child Research, of the National Institute for Mental Health, Redl, of course, writes as a clinician but he makes an attempt to distinguish between healthy defiance which is a part of the growth process of normal youth, defiance which is neurotic, and defiance which is a concomitant of delinquent behavior socially derived.

Writing under the title of "Our Troubles with Defiant Youth," [10] Redl remarks that defiance itself cannot be equated with delinquency or even with emotional disturbance, in the pathological use of the term. He points out emphatically, however, that some types of defiance are

[6] Howard Lane. "The Meaning of Disorder Among Youth." *Education*, 76:214-17, December 1955.

[7] Tappan, *op. cit.*, p. 681.

[8] Beck, *op. cit.*, p. 65.

[9] As quoted in *Time*, December 6, 1954, p. 64-65.

[10] Fritz Redl. "Our Troubles with Defiant Youth." *Children*, January-February, 1955. p. 5-9.

indeed indicators of behavior which is an expression of deep seated emotional conflicts, or behavior which is delinquent.

Of interest to teachers, school administrators, and all others concerned with youth problems is Redl's helpful distinction between defiance that is a normal part of growth and defiance that is pathological.

"Developmental defiance," to use his words for the normal defiance of growth, develops because youth must not only learn to adjust and readjust to the demands of his environment, including his associations with all age groups, types and kinds of people, but because at the same time, he has to maintain his own integrity as a person. Conformity to social demands, which is essential for fitting in, is, Redl believes, one phase of the development of an adequate person. But healthy rebellion is an equally important aspect of adequacy. This latter rebellion is the stuff out of which integrity grows—the willingness to stand up and fight for what is considered "right" by the youngster even in the face of pressures from his own group or from his adult associates, who are sometimes off on the wrong track as surely as is the youth.[11]

Rebellion, Redl reminds us, is an important part of preparation for the independence of the youth as he moves toward the dependability of adulthood.

Moreover, Harry Estill Moore has made the point that without the rebel, or the one who is willing to "break the cake of custom," as Bagehot put it, there would be no creativity unleashed in new ways of behaving, new invention and scientific discoveries. "Essentially," he writes, "creativity toward progress (or maturation) comes only when there is dissatisfaction with the customary, with the status quo, strong enough to push toward new solutions. . . ."[12]

Defiance, Redl again stresses, shows itself in the opposite of the coward, the over-conformist, the spineless character who turns into a person with no independence of opinion or action and who may, in fact, become the epitome of Whyte's Organization Man.[13] While defiance and rebellion in the youth may not be comfortable for the adults in his social field, as Kurt Lewin has described it, these same adults must take care not to destroy, for their own immediate comfort, the essence of integrity and creativity which may be of tremendous service to a nation faced with a "space age."

[11] Ibid., p. 7.
[12] "What Is Creative Living in Modern America?" Educational Leadership, October 1956. p. 28.
[13] William H. Whyte, Jr. The Organization Man. New York: Simon and Schuster, 1956.

"Defiance as Warping"

Examination of distinctions in defiant behavior in no way minimizes what Redl describes as "defiance as warping." Warping may be either social or emotional. Unwarranted behavior or apparently unprovoked behavior is a danger signal of the rebellious or delinquent child in the making. The rebellious child may display his problem by acting out or by seemingly aimless wandering, in fact or in fancy, and it may be expressed either in destructive behavior or in withdrawal. Here the only way to attack the problem is to see that the child gets to the person trained to uncover and determine what is back of his diseased behavior.

"The defiant ego," described by Redl, shows itself in uncontrolled impulsiveness. Destruction is enjoyed. Fun is an immediate need and any behavior in which the person wants to indulge becomes "fun."

. . . Either they have not developed that "voice from within" that would make them feel bad about "fun" that is unjustly had at somebody else's expense; or they have developed very skillful tricks of putting that "voice" out of commission should it tend to interfere. Diagnosis, however, is not easy. . . .[14]

To quote Redl further:

Clinically speaking, then, we have to look a few inches below the surface before we can know what problems in any specific "defiant act" really are. Where behavior falls into the category of "developmental defiance," it presents us with an educational challenge, but we must not be fooled into regarding it as "delinquency." [15]

And it might well be added that care must be taken not to equate delinquent behavior, destructive to the group, with normal and healthy aggression.

Two other areas of defiance are noted by Redl and demand consideration for understanding the necessary distinctions between the normal and the problem aspects of youth behavior. "Reactive defiance," he states, is not necessarily surfacing of a degenerate personality, but may be a protest against treatment which, to quote, "shouldn't happen to a dog." An example of defiance of this nature is found when a youth fights back and may even kill because of constant mistreatment and brutality by an alcoholic or criminal father or wanton mother. In a less dramatic form, it is observed when children are bored to the point of satiation by an incompetent teacher and demoralization sets in. Reactive defiance, then, demands a double-edged examination. What

[14] Redl, *op. cit.*, p. 8.
[15] *Ibid.*, p. 7.

is wrong with the child? And even more important, what is wrong with what adults are doing to him? Redl explains that the "defiant ego" in action is the type of affliction which can be described as "delinquency" even though the actual behavior may not violate any law. Early diagnosis, further study and research toward effective diagnosis and treatment of these children and youth are now Redl's major assignment.

While Albert K. Cohen discusses the delinquent subculture of boy gangs rather than behavior problems as such, his description is relevant in light of the studies cited above. He describes the delinquent subculture as "non-utilitarian, malicious, and negativistic." [16] Stealing by gang members, he notes, is not in line at all with stealing by the adult criminal. Criminals want what they steal or the money from it. The delinquent, on the other hand, has no such motivation. Gang stealing, as Cohen cryptically says, is stealing "for the hell of it." Paul Tappan describes this same phenomenon as the "sport motive." Stealing is engaged in by delinquent boys for status, and Cohen remarks that *why* stealing gives status is a good question!

Malice, Cohen believes, is apparent throughout delinquent behavior. He holds that definite pleasure is attained from the discomfort of others—a similar observation to Redl's. Delight is taken in defiance of taboos, and the gang delinquent takes keen pleasure in expressing hostility toward adults and "terrorizing good children." Teachers and their rules are not to be evaded but they are to be flouted.

Within this pattern, the elements of active spite, contempt, ridicule and defiance are apparent. Moreover, Cohen believes that delinquency tends to turn upside down what is considered acceptable in behavior. The delinquent will tend to describe himself as "just plain mean."

Cohen remarks that versatility in behavior distinguishes the delinquent. He will steal but also his stealing goes hand in hand with malicious mischief, vandalism, trespassing and truancy. This is described as a fusion of versatility in behavior with malice in intent.[17] Delinquent gang members are marked for lack of long-term goals or ideals. They have little or no interest in activities which take skill, knowledge and planning. They want to do what they want to do right at the moment. This finding has been borne out by a recent descriptive study [18] of El Paso, Texas, gangs by Father Harold J. Rahm and

[16] Albert K. Cohen. *Delinquent Boys: The Culture of the Gang.* Glencoe, Illinois: The Free Press, 1955. p. 25.

[17] *Ibid.,* p. 28-29.

[18] Father Harold J. Rahm and Robert Weber. *Office in the Alley.* Austin, Texas: The Hogg Foundation for Mental Health, The University of Texas, 1958.

Robert Weber. These youngsters are "impatient and impetuous," to quote the colorful writing of Cohen again.

Delinquent behavior as described here is close to the expression of "defiant egos" as portrayed by Fritz Redl. Emphasis on group autonomy rather than upon the individual delinquent must be kept in mind, Cohen points out. Gang members resist restraint at school, at home, through other agencies, and they fight regulation on any front.[19]

No one would accept this description of the behavior of members of the delinquent gang subculture as indicative of the behavior of all delinquents, but it does express in active terms, behavior which is evident among a large segment of children and youth with severe social and emotional problems expressed through delinquency.

Robert L. Sutherland points out different patterns of delinquent behavior in an unusual description in "Delinquency and Mental Health." [20] Sutherland talks about a pair of "Toms," each with different manifestations of problems and each expressing them in ways which would be called delinquent.

Tom learned to use a switch-blade early. He could draw and snap as quickly as anyone in the gang. Not that knife fighting was a daily occurrence; simply that carrying a "good knife" had become a custom of that gang. It was handy in case of "emergency." [21]

The second Tom is described as follows:

With Tom it was a little different. He belonged to the gang and talked big in their presence but never could be found if real danger came.

Instead he used his knife as a bullying weapon on smaller "punks." He loved to overtake a little boy or girl, snap his knife, and force the child against a wall, using the words and techniques of a bully but so far stopping short of physical harm.[22]

The actions of the first Tom may be attributed to his subculture even as Cohen uses the term. Sutherland states that this Tom could scarcely be described as an emotional misfit in that he is "hale, hearty, vigorous, adjusted to his peers, to their aspirations, their folkways of living, and their system of rewards." But he is a delinquent in that his entire subculture is at war with the larger culture.

The second Tom, Sutherland indicates, is also a delinquent of the emotionally unbalanced type. He picks on small children. He has a

---

[19] Cohen, op. cit., p. 31.

[20] Robert L. Sutherland. "Delinquency and Mental Health." Federal Probation, March 1957. Reprint, Austin, Texas: The Hogg Foundation for Mental Health, The University of Texas. (Page numbers refer to the reprint.)

[21] Ibid., p. 1.

[22] Ibid., p. 1.

latent yellow streak which keeps him from going all the way with the gang and yet he has learned his skills from the gang. Moreover, traces of sadism are discernible in this Tom, and his behavior shows problems of emotional adjustment complicated by environmental factors. Sutherland writes, "According to society, Tom was a delinquent when he followed the gang. According to the gang, he was delinquent when he set out on pathological conduct of his own." [23]

Sutherland then throws the behavior of these two Toms against the definition of mental health by Marie Jahoda, in paraphrase:

. . . mental health is the condition of the personality which includes active adjustment to meet and overcome problems, a maintenance of inner stability, even when faced with new conditions, and a realistic judgment of the world in which we live and of ourselves as a part of that world.[24]

The first Tom, Robert L. Sutherland indicates, is mentally ill on the one count that his subculture is unrealistic and antisocial in relation to the larger community. The second Tom, on the other hand, not only fails on this count since he, too, is associated with a gang, but he also misses out in his adjustment "to his peer group and shows signs of emotional confusion and instability." [25]

Sutherland concludes that cultural delinquency—the delinquent pattern of the first Tom—can be found on various levels of social class in a community though it is far more prevalent among the low income areas. Delinquency patterns of the second Tom, with their high emotional content, can be found on all levels of society. Cultural delinquency is the province of anthropologists and sociologists. Psychiatrists, psychoanalysts, psychologists and psychiatric social workers have developed the "tools" and "concepts" for the study of the "emotional delinquent." [26]

Characteristics of Deviant Behavior

An excellent summary of the foregoing analyses comes from a study by R. L. Jenkins and Sylvia Glickman under the title, "Common Syndromes in Child Psychiatry, I. Deviant Behavior Traits," [27] from the

[23] Ibid., p. 1.
[24] Ibid., p. 2. From Marie Jahoda, "Toward a Social Psychology of Mental Health." In Arnold M. Rose, editor, Mental Health and Mental Disorder, New York: W. W. Norton & Company, 1955. p. 558-66. Copyright, 1955, by W. W. Norton & Company, Inc.
[25] Ibid., p. 2.
[26] Ibid., p. 2.
[27] Reprinted from R. L. Jenkins and Sylvia Glickman, "Common Syndromes in Child Psychiatry, I. Deviant Behavior Traits," The American Journal of Orthopsychiatry, 16:248-49, 1946.

American Journal of Orthopsychiatry. These two scholars based a research study of clinical cases on two previous studies which had attempted to make a classification of behavior in deviant children and youth.[28] They note that classical psychiatry did tend toward too rigid classification of personality problems, but they argue that a flexible classification is useful and does not necessarily make for rigidity. Rather, flexible classification proves an aid in early discovery of need, and for teachers it furnishes a guidepost for referral. It is interesting to see how closely the descriptions of behavior by these two scholars parallel those of Redl, Cohen and Sutherland.

The Jenkins and Hewitt study had organized its findings around three types of behavior in children: the over-inhibited, the unsocialized, and the socialized delinquent or the pseudo-socialized.

In tables of behavior characteristics of these three groups of children, based on the Jenkins and Hewitt study and tested by intercorrelations with over 100 behavior traits from the Luton Ackerson book, and as demonstrated in their own clinical patients, Jenkins and Glickman present the following descriptive designations: [29]

The Over-Inhibited

Boys	Girls
Sensitiveness over specific fact	Inferiority feelings
Inferiority feelings	Depressed or discouraged attitudes
Depressed or discouraged attitudes	Sensitiveness
Worry over specific fact	Sensitiveness over specific fact
Mental conflict	Daydreaming
Unhappy manner	Crying spells
Psychoneurotic trends	Seclusiveness.
Sensitiveness	
Seclusiveness	
Daydreaming	

Needless to point out, not one over-inhibited child displays all of these behavior patterns. However, this listing does offer evidence for teachers and others that special concern should be manifested by them when there is an obvious constellation of such behavior in a

---

[28] The previous studies were R. L. Jenkins and Lester Hewitt, "Types of Personality Structure Encountered in Child Guidance Clinics," *The American Journal of Orthopsychiatry,* January 1944; and Luton Ackerson, *Child Behavior Problems,* Volume II, Behavior Research Fund Monograph, Chicago, Illinois: The University of Chicago Press, 1942.

[29] Jenkins and Glickman. *op. cit.* p. 248.

given child. This same precaution holds, of course, for the designation of possible patterns of action which follow for the unsocialized and the pseudo-socialized child.

The Unsocialized [30]

Boys	Girls
Disturbing influence in school	Violence
Violence	Fighting
Fighting	Incorrigibility
Quarrelsomeness	Temper tantrums
Destructiveness	Defiant attitude
Incorrigibility	Disobedience
Boastfulness	Disturbing influence in school
Teasing other children	Rudeness
Exclusion from school	Quarrelsomeness
Unpopularity	Exclusion from school
	Lying
	Unpopularity
	Leading others into bad conduct
	Destructiveness
	"Queerness."

Girl-Variant Group

Boastfulness	Unpopularity
Violence	Egocentricity
Bossiness	Selfishness
Temper tantrums	Changeable moods
	"Spoiled child."

It is interesting to observe how many qualities the unsocialized child and the second "Tom" of the Sutherland discussion have in common. Moreover, Cohen would describe the unsocialized child who becomes delinquent as a child or youth with psychogenic origin of behavior problems. Neither of these men took into account the young girl in their discussion of the above qualities, possibly because overt delinquency among girls usually is defined in the category of sex delinquency and is low in number as compared with all delinquency among boys.

Finally the "socialized delinquent" of Jenkins and Glickman, the first "Tom" of Sutherland, and the delinquent from the subculture of Cohen have much in common:

[30] *Ibid.,* p. 249.

The Socialized Delinquent or Pseudo-socialized [31]

Boys	Girls
Stealing	Staying out late at night
Truancy from home	Truancy from home
Truancy from school	Truancy from school
Police arrest	Police arrest
Staying out late at night	Lying
Associating with bad	Sex delinquency
companions	Stealing
"Running around with a gang"	Overinterest in the opposite sex
Smoking and loitering	Incorrigibility
Lying	Associating with bad
Incorrigibility	companions
Leading others into bad	Loitering.
conduct	

That delinquent behavior is not simple is an obvious conclusion from the research and theoretical studies discussed herein. Delinquency may arise from different sources within the environment or within the person. Nor can delinquency or predelinquency be scientifically diagnosed as yet, though numerous prediction studies are being attempted. Difficulties beset early categorization because such behavior is not readily distinguishable from the occasional surface behavior of children and youth who will never become delinquent and because it is extremely difficult to isolate and measure all the factors involved in the development of the delinquent.

Some Beginnings of Theories of Prediction

This discussion would not be adequate without taking note of the study by Sheldon and Eleanor Glueck which has been published under the title, *Unraveling Juvenile Delinquency*.[32]

In a review of this book, Sheldon Glueck stressed the need for what he calls "an exact scientific approach to research in delinquency." [33] He and his wife attempted to put this belief into action in gathering comparative data for their study between matched groups of delinquents in an institution and nondelinquents outside an institution. Moreover, they indicate, their study emphasizes the plurality of causes

[31] *Ibid.*, p. 250-51.

[32] Reprinted by permission of the publishers and The Commonwealth Fund from Sheldon and Eleanor Glueck. *Unraveling Juvenile Delinquency.* Cambridge, Massachusetts: Harvard University Press, 1950. p. 281-82

[33] Sheldon Glueck. *Harvard Educational Review* 23: 17-32; 1952.

of delinquency, but, more important, offers a basis for prediction of possible incidence "with about 90 percent accuracy." They write, "The signals of persistent delinquency flash their warning before puberty," and, therefore, early testing of children to determine delinquency proneness is indicated as a part of the testing program of public schools.

Perhaps no recent statement has caused more controversy than the Gluecks' "causal formulation" or law. They indicate the mass of delinquents can be distinguished from nondelinquents by the following characteristics:

1. Physically, in being essentially mesomorphic in constitution—solidly built, closely knit, muscular physical structure

2. Temperamentally, in being restless, energetic, impulsive, extroverted, aggressive, destructive, often sadistic

3. In attitude, by displaying hostility, defiance, resentfulness, suspiciousness, stubbornness; socially assertive, adventurous, unconventional, nonsubmissive to authority

4. Psychologically, in having tendencies to direct and concrete action and thought rather than use of the symbolic; less methodical in approach to problems

5. Socio-culturally, in having been reared in homes where there is little understanding, affection, stability or moral fibre and by parents usually unfit as guides and protectors, or according to psychoanalytic theory, not of the quality of personality to be ego-ideals for their children.[34]

The Gluecks indicate that while in unusual cases any one of the above characteristics may produce delinquency, their law or theory is based on the conviction that there has to be an interaction between all of these forces to develop a delinquent.

Youngsters raised in environments "little controlled and culturally inconsistent," the Gluecks state, give quick expression to their "untamed impulses" and use to excess their "uninhibited energy" to set a pattern early in their lives which is delinquent and which will, in all probability, become more or less permanent. Environments conducive to such developmental forces are usually the underprivileged slum communities in larger cities.[35]

In a careful analysis of the Gluecks' research, Sol Rubin [36] offers what appears to him to be two glaring errors in their method of

[34] Glueck and Glueck, op. cit., p. 281-82.
[35] Ibid., p. 281-82.
[36] Sol Rubin. "Unraveling Juvenile Delinquency, I. Illusions in a Research Project Using Matched Pairs." American Journal of Sociology, September 1951. p. 108-109. Published by University of Chicago Press.

arriving at results. Comparing groups of delinquent boys in an institution with a group of boys outside the institution who are nondelinquent is, according to Rubin, comparing the incomparable. He states that such comparison has long been regarded as inconsistent and relatively impossible. What is really under study in these two situations is a group of institutionalized offenders, who provide information about youth who are institutionalized; and a second group of non-offenders, non-institutionalized, who, in turn, give data on themselves.

Moreover, Rubin points out, the Gluecks did not take into account broader social causation than the family. As he states it:

The slums are characterized not only by strongly criminogenic elements but also by forces strongly supporting lawful behavior. The latter are positive community attributes and family, group, and individual resources, which operate to protect some individuals better than others. Chance, too, plays a part in the selection of youngsters fated to be delinquent: the separation into delinquents and non-delinquents is not always a basic separation, not the sharp differentiation which the categories imply. A change in administrative policy may mean a change in the delinquency rate. In a slum, delinquent behavior for some may frequently be not unnatural, but rather a natural choice; it is not the only choice; and lawful behavior is likewise not the only choice. . . .[37]

In a second article of the critique of the Gluecks' study, Albert J. Reiss, Jr., points out the limited perspective of the study in what he calls the "sociological factors." [38] He is particularly concerned with the Gluecks' statement from a cursory statistical presentation that "birds of a feather flock together" in delinquent gangs. As he notes, the Gluecks neglect the possibility that delinquent associates with other youngsters serve as easy and accessible ego-ideals. Moreover, the delinquent gang exercises real control over its members. Overlooked are "certain systematic aspects of delinquency" which can be and are learned with delinquents as the teachers of non-delinquent youth.

Unacceptable to sociologists, Reiss stresses, is the belief that delinquency is inevitable because of a person's physical and psychologic equipment, or the "congeniality" of his biologic tendencies to an antisocial culture. Fixity of character by the time a child is six is not accepted by sociologists—and, it may be added, many psychologists and psychiatrists as well. Experiences throughout the life history of a person must be taken into account as they may lead toward or away from delinquency.

[37] *Ibid.*, p. 108.

[38] Albert J. Reiss, Jr. Unraveling Juvenile Delinquency, II. An Appraisal of the Research Methods." *American Journal of Sociology*, September 1951. p. 117. Published by University of Chicago Press.

To a sociologist, Reiss says, more important considerations include answers to such questions as: "What is the role of the social group in developing delinquency-oriented character structure?" "Given a delinquency-oriented character structure, what are the environmental conditions which dispose him toward and against delinquency?" "In what ways can the milieu restructure the 'delinquency-oriented' characters?" [39]

Finding answers to these problems, Reiss concludes, would point out the roles of families, of churches, of schools—all primary groups; and it would take into account secondary institutions in the wider community as well, with these having an important share in the structuring of personality of the child and in enforcing behavior within a set of accepted standards. After all, Reiss stresses, behavior in line with broad over-all values, goals and standards in the larger social group is the index of "success."

Research on the validation of the Glueck Prediction Scale was undertaken by the New York City Youth Board. Marie Duffin, the board's deputy executive director, revealed at the 52nd annual convention of the Boys' Clubs of America that the board began an investigation in 1952 and that this was based on five factors of family relationship. These factors included: discipline of the boy by the father; supervision of the boy by the mother; affection of the father for the boy; affection of the mother for the boy; and cohesiveness of the family. Validity of the formula was tested on 303 Negro and Puerto Rican boys.[40] Results of this study were published by the New York City Youth Board in July 1957 as "An Experiment in the Validation of the Glueck Prediction Scale."

Sol Rubin, in the critical article discussed above, offers an eclectic approach to the problem of prevention of delinquency that is appropriate here. He refers to the findings of the St. Paul experiment in child welfare and its basic philosophy as indicative of a comprehensive approach to a complex problem.[41]

[39] *Ibid.*, p. 117.

[40] "Detection Test Told." *The Austin* (Texas) *American*, May 8, 1958, p. 10. In addition three other publications of the New York City Youth Board are: *Teenage Gangs*, 1957; *Reaching Teen-Agers Through Group Work and Recreation Programs*, 1954; and *Reaching the Group; An Analysis of Group Work Methods Used with Teen-Agers*, Monograph #4, 1956.

[41] Sybil A. Stone, Elsa Castendyck and Harold B. Hanson. *Children in the Community: The St. Paul Experiment in Child Welfare*. Children's Bureau Publication, No. 317. Washington, D.C.: U.S. Department of Health, Education, and Welfare, 1946. See a similar approach in H. Aubrey Elliott with Bert K. Smith, *Pillars of Support*, Austin, Texas: The Hogg Foundation for Mental Health, The University of Texas, 1956.

The St. Paul study worked from the basic premise that each child must be treated as a "whole child," and that his problems need to be seen as a unit even if they are numerous and varied. Moreover, it was found that minor problems of children may be easily and early discovered, and if community services for children are effectively coordinated so that these youngsters get the help they need, serious consequences are avoided.

For prevention of serious behavior problems, the St. Paul study emphasized that not only do social work agencies need to coordinate their services, but that all other agencies in a community, such as the schools, health services, recreational and law enforcement agencies, should be closely related for maximum preventive endeavor. Rubin points out that the acceptance of this basic premise—of seeing the child and his problems as a whole and utilizing all available resources, either directly or indirectly, for his needs—is of primary importance for any community which is seriously interested in delinquency prevention. Rubin concludes:

The foregoing are attributes of a rational crime-prevention program, which considers the whole child; which takes his behavior as sharing in and reflecting his own, his family's, his community's life; which recognizes that he may develop critical difficulties at any time—at or before school entrance or any time thereafter. His conduct is determined not only by his own attitudes and character and those of his family and companions, but, not least, by the attitudes and character of the community and its agencies. . . .[42]

William C. Kvaraceus remarks that in recent years there has been a growing attempt to develop tools and techniques for prediction of delinquency, but that, so far, these are useful only to research persons interested in further development of them.[43] Among those worth further study, he includes the Glueck Prediction Tables, the Minnesota Multiphasic Personality Inventory, the Porteus Maze Test, the Washburne Social Adjustment Inventory, the Stogdill Behavior Cards, the KD Proneness Scale and Check List, and the Personal Index Test.

Kvaraceus summarizes the difficulties of all such attempts at predicting future delinquency by stating that there is no clear-cut dichotomy between delinquent and nondelinquent. Behavior occurs on a continuum, he indicates, and delinquent behavior also follows this pattern displaying varying degrees of seriousness and of habituation. Moreover, he reiterates, as do all scholars in the field, that only

[42] Rubin, op. cit., p. 113-14.

[43] William C. Kvaraceus. "Prediction Studies of Delinquent Behavior." The Personnel and Guidance Journal, November 1955. p. 147-49.

a very small and selected group of offenders are apprehended and are, therefore, countable as delinquent. These represent a highly selected group, and when those in institutions are chosen for study, this is indeed a "hardy breed" of delinquent and quite different from others who are occasional deviants.[44]

Would-be predictors in the field of juvenile delinquency are warned by Kvaraceus that they need to define carefully the peculiar characteristics of the delinquent population which they propose to study and to state these characteristics with precision. Samples for study have to be drawn with greater care, as was also stressed by Rubin. Most important, research workers in prediction have the imperative to restrict use of their data and interpretation of it to the type of delinquent who made up their sample.[45]

These comments from Kvaraceus, Rubin, Reiss, and others indicate that social and behavioral scientists, as well as clinicians, are far from being able to predict who will become delinquent and who will not. More important than data from current prediction studies is the acquisition of an effective working knowledge of the dynamics of human behavior and of how to apply this to the problems which arise in the behavior of youth.[46]

[44] *Ibid.*, p. 147.
[45] *Ibid.*, p. 148.
[46] See also: *Report to the Congress on Juvenile Delinquency.* Washington, D. C.: U. S. Department of Health, Education, and Welfare; Children's Bureau; and National Institute of Mental Health, 1960.

CHAPTER 4

Delinquency—Multiple Theories of Multiple Causes

DELINQUENCY is now recognized as the end product of a variety of situations, attitudes, motives, role definitions, self-images and personality characteristics. Theories of the causes of delinquency are therefore equally complex.

Robert K. Merton, a sociologist whose own thesis will be discussed, has crystallized this complexity by describing the concept "delinquency" as a "blanket" which obscures rather than clarifies the behavior thus labeled. "Juvenile delinquents," he points out, tend to become a "type." This forces behavioral scientists—psychiatrists, sociologists, anthropologists and psychologists—toward an attempt at a single, all-encompassing theory of juvenile delinquency.

The basic problem for theories of delinquency, Merton states, is an explanation of various types of deviant behavior in a variety of situations. Therefore, he believes, there is valid reason for the development of *theories* of delinquency rather than striving for *a theory* which would, of necessity, block out diversity through an attempt toward uniformity.[1]

Theory in relation to social problems, mathematical formulation, or any scientific research has major services to perform. The more important in this immediate instance is that theory offers opportunity to learn more about basic factors in a problem and to gain insight as to its many facets, implications, and variety of possibilities which need investigation for its solution.

From a research point of view, theory makes possible an ordered framework or orientation from which to proceed in gathering empirical data or facts and against which to test these data. Also, when a theory

[1] Robert K. Merton. *New Perspectives for Research on Juvenile Delinquency,* Helen L. Witmer and Ruth Kotinsky, editors. Children's Bureau Publication, No. 356. Washington, D.C.: United States Department of Health, Education, and Welfare, 1956. p. 27-28.

is developed and stated, other scholars have an opportunity to examine it carefully, analyze it against their own knowledge and backgrounds, and are either stimulated toward new and otherwise unexplored ways of thinking about a problem or are critical to the advantage of clarifying their own thinking.[2]

This discussion will proceed from the psychoanalytic, or highly individualized, theory of delinquency to the broad cultural and social approach which has incorporated within it the psychological, psychoanalytic, and sociological conceptions concerning the imperative problem.

A Psychoanalytic Theory of Delinquency

Freudian psychoanalytic theory has invaded many problem areas of human behavior and the area of delinquency is no exception. This theory holds that children are born into the world with instinctual or inborn antisocial drives. These drives must be brought under control by the integration of socially accepted behavior patterns and value structures into the ego and superego. To achieve these ends, the person is in conflict with his instinctive nature and the social and emotional demands of his culture. To become social, the person must learn to "control" his "'asocial'" drives and desires.

E. R. Eissler, a psychoanalyst with a religious overtone of his own, and an extreme adherence to classical psychoanalytic theory, equates this struggle within man with the struggle between Good and Evil which began when Adam and Eve ate from the Tree of Knowledge. The first crime, as Eissler calls it, forced man to serve simultaneously his body, or his instinctual drives, his external world or its standards of behavior, and his conscience or his internalized values and ideals. To quote:

Driven by an inexplicable urge to create ethical and moral values, an urge of equal intensity drives man to destroy and falsify these same values. However lofty his goals and ardent his strivings, the full record of each man's life is disfigured with the strain of acts and desires irreconcilable with his convictions of what is good and just.[3]

From this frame of reference, it follows that Eissler and others with similar orientation assign "the generic term delinquency" to "all thoughts, actions, desires and strivings which deviate from moral and

[2] See the section "What Is a Theory?" in Calvin S. Hall and Gardner Lindzey, *Theories of Personality*, New York: John Wiley and Sons, Inc., 1957. p. 10-15.

[3] E. R. Eissler, editor. *Searchlights on Delinquency*. New York: International Universities Press, Inc., 1955. p. 3.

ethical principles." His all encompassing definition, he points out, is in disagreement with other psychiatric schools which believe that delinquency may come from environmental stresses and pressures, and that delinquent acts vary with tradition, time in history, and local customs.[4]

As is indicated, Eissler offers as his primary definition of delinquency that which "infringes upon values" either in thoughts, feelings or behavior, and this, at one time or another in a life span, would seem to include almost everyone except an angel on earth. The behavior of a criminal or delinquent, according to him, is purely reaction to instinctual desires without restraint of conscience. Pleasure and the drive for immediate satisfaction are the only motivations for such behavior.[5]

Eissler continues, since the delinquent is asocial, and has no feeling of attachment for anyone—no value structure for control of his behavior—the first step in his socialization, or in the development of a functioning ego and superego, is the establishment of a ". . . tight, fool-proof attachment between psychoanalyst and the delinquent in the shortest possible time. . . ."[6] The therapist, then, must become the delinquent's ideal if he is to stand a chance of getting a hold on the deviant. The analyst assumes the role of protector of the delinquent against himself and takes the place of an unfailing helper and friend.[7] Eissler notes that the effective delinquent has a "keen, alert" mind and becomes a "shrewd amateur psychologist, an expert of the surface of the human mind, and an excellent manipulator of people. . . ."[8] This observation will later be corroborated in observations by Fritz Redl and David Wineman in their theory of the delinquent ego.

Delinquency, as other deviant behavior, according to the psychoanalyst, grows out of frustrations suffered as a growing child. Delinquency is a form of withdrawal from normal behavior and values of a society, and is an adaptive mechanism in the face of extreme frustration even as there is withdrawal from reality in psychoses. However, Eissler warns that delinquencies are distinctive in themselves and are a unique set of disorders.[9] Eissler concludes his discussion of delinquency by saying:

To a certain extent it can be rightly claimed that the delinquent is a

[4] Ibid., p. 4.
[5] Ibid., p. 7.
[6] Ibid., p. 17.
[7] Ibid., p. 19.
[8] Ibid., p. 18.
[9] Ibid., p. 24-25

distorted model of normal behavior since the pleasure principle is maintained to a degree pleasing to the delinquent without endangering the patient's survival and freedom if he is smart enough to select as his hunting ground one among those in which society permits the free growth of condoned delinquency.[10]

A Theory of Identity Diffusion and Psychosocial Moratorium

Erik H. Erikson, representing another psychoanalytic school less classically Freudian, has described "human growth from the point of view of the conflicts, inner and outer, which the healthy personality weathers, emerging and re-emerging with an increased sense of inner unity, with an increase of good judgment, and an increase in the capacity to do well, according to the standards of those who are significant to him. . . ."[11]

Erikson includes in these growth stages the acquisition of basic trust of others out of the dependent relationship of infancy and early childhood to mother or mother substitutes. Autonomy or independence is the stage of discovery of self as a separate being rather than as an extension of the mother figure. Initiative is developed, as is industry, if growth is healthy as contrasted to feelings of guilt and inferiority. These are accomplishments of childhood.

When adolescence is reached, crises in growth include the development of ego identity as contrasted with ego diffusion, a concept which bears heavily upon Erikson's theory of delinquency. Intimacy comes into the life of the person when he is sure *who* he is and *how* he is regarded by others. In young maturity the "crisis of generativity" is reached, which is expressed in procreation but also in creativity and productivity on many fronts. Finally, the development of integrity is attained in the healthy personality. Integrity assumes the acceptance of "a sense of comradeship with men and women" of the past, of the present, and of the future with "no fear of death, no feeling of despair at the shortness of the life span." Erikson writes, "Ego integrity, therefore, implies an emotional integration which permits participation by 'followership' as well as acceptance of the responsibility of leadership: both must be learned and practiced."[12] Then, he continues, children

---

[10] *Ibid.*, p. 25.

[11] Erik H. Erikson. "Growth and Crisis of the 'Healthy Personality.'" *Symposium on the Healthy Personality*, Milton J. E. Senn, editor. New York: Josiah Macy Jr. Foundation, 1950. p. 91-146.

[12] *Ibid.*, p. 144.

and adults reflect the quality of the milieu or environment in which they grow, a statement which is a far cry from classical analytic theory. "To develop a child with a healthy personality, a parent must be a genuine person in a genuine milieu." [13] Here he takes into account both the persons in the environment and the environment itself as active agents in the behavior of growing children.

Along the way in the development of some, ego identity does not materialize. "Ego identity" to Erikson is achieved when there is a coalescence within the personality of how one sees himself and how well this corresponds to how others see him. Or to state this same observation in a slightly different way, Erikson says, ". . . the individual comes to feel most himself where he means most to others—to those others who have come to mean most to him." [14] Marie Jahoda uses somewhat this same concept in her definition of positive mental health when she states a realistic judgment of the world in which one lives plus a realistic judgment of oneself in that world is essential to mental health.[15] Still a simpler way to express ego identity is to say it has been achieved "when we see ourselves as others see us."

"Ego diffusion" results when the personality does not achieve this reality vision of himself in his relation to others. The youth in such a state is not sure how he feels about himself, and is certainly unsure of how he appears to others and how they feel about him. Theoretically, Erikson states, "the study of identity diffusion as a crisis of youth includes that of juvenile delinquency." [16]

Attaining and continuing ego identity, Erikson indicates, is a lifelong process. However, in its essence, this is an achievement of adolescence. When a youth, making his last step into maturity, has no sense of being recognized by others in the same way he sees himself; when he feels he does not mean much to others who do mean much to him—then "a transitory disturbance" in personality development arises. This may produce not only "a malignant episode" such as a quick series of delinquent acts which are soon over, but it may result in basic personality defect. When the latter occurs, then comes "acute or chronic identity diffusion." [17]

Delinquent behavior, of course, is only one manifestation of such

[13] Ibid., p. 145.

[14] Erik H. Erikson. New Perspectives for Research on Juvenile Delinquency. Helen L. Witmer and Ruth Kotinsky, editors. p. 4.

[15] Marie Jahoda. "Toward a Social Psychology of Mental Health." Mental Health and Mental Disorder. Arnold M. Rose, editor. New York: W. W. Norton & Company, 1955. p. 566. Copyright, 1955, by W. W. Norton & Company, Inc.

[16] Erik H. Erikson, op. cit., p. 56.

[17] Ibid., p. 4.

diffusion. Others include the development of neurotic or, in extreme cases, psychotic symptoms.

Erikson points out how important it is for young persons to be recognized as individuals of worth and predictability by others of their age, but more influential is recognition by *important* adults. However, he warns that in this particular day recognition of youth seems to be oriented toward a conception of them as being of little worth, of disgraceful, unsocial behavior, of dilatory practices, of delinquent tendencies if not of delinquent acts. He believes that too much recognition of youth as a group which arouses "displeasure and discomfort" is now given at a critical moment in their development.

Erikson continues:

. . . Then the community, or some important people in it, will more or less explicitly suggest to the young person that he change in ways that to him do not add up to anything "identical with himself." The reasons for this feeling on the young person's part, only an analysis of his unconscious identity fragments could reveal. To the community, however, the desirable change is conceived of as a matter of good will and of will power, while resistance to change is perceived as a matter of bad will and of inferiority, hereditary or otherwise. Thus the community underestimates, at one time, to what extent a long, intricate history has restricted a youth's choices of identity formation, and at another, to what extent the community could, if it only would, still help determine a youth's destiny within these choices.[18]

Erikson offers a second important concept for the clarification of delinquent behavior in what he calls the *psychosocial moratorium*. Moratorium is used in the usual sense of a granted delay in the assumption of an obligation. This clinician applies the term moratorium to the postponement of the assumption of adult commitments, obligations and responsibilities. He points out that this is even more than a delay in taking on the dependability of adulthood in that it is both made possible, and sanctioned by, a permissiveness in society for unresponsibility coinciding with "a provocative playfulness on the part of youth." [19]

This social fact has been indicated by many students of youth and their developmental problems. Postponement of marriage until completion of education and employment offers a period of relationships between the sexes without the commitment or responsibility of marriage. Extension of education through the "teen" years offers escape from occupational obligations. Community organization for worth-

[18] *Ibid.*, p. 5.
[19] *Ibid.*, p. 5.

while and valuable accomplishments rarely takes into account the possible contribution of intelligent, energetic and capable youth.

Variations in how youth react to this moratorium are many; and Erikson comments that some gifted adult eccentrics never seem to take on their share of mature accountability for behavior.

Moratorium from adult responsibility is institutionalized by certain societies and cultures, Erikson says, and most of the adventuresome behavior of the adolescent period is within the sanction of the values of the culture. However, behavior during this period of moratorium may be outside of the acceptable, and when this occurs, delinquency is one form of deviation.

Erikson offers a unique warning concerning the tendency in this country to send youth of deviant behavior to psychiatrists for "treatment" as an alternative to bringing them to acceptance and participation in behavior which has become standard and universally recognized as acceptable. He believes "treatment itself" may be used as a form of psychosocial moratorium which will destroy the necessity for adolescents to pass through this growth stage toward sound ego identity and adult responsibility. Erikson would not, of course, advocate that psychiatric treatment should not be made available for youth in trouble, but he seems to imply that "treatment" should be toward the norms of the culture and should not be utilized for escape from the consequences of one's behavior.[20] As Edward J. Shoben, Jr. has stated, three major facets of the normal healthy personality are self-control through postponement of immediate satisfactions for long-term goals; self responsibility in taking the consequences for one's behavior; and social responsibility because of the intricate relationship of the person to his society.[21] Erikson states further, "At any rate, our consideration should include not only research in juvenile delinquency as a clinical picture, but also research in the institutions that provide specific moratoria at the price of the individual's acceptance of a certain status, such as 'patient.'"[22]

Erikson also points out that juvenile delinquency itself may be an attempt, in its organized form, to create a pathological institution which assures a negative kind of psychosocial moratorium from adult social responsibility. He adds that it is probable that delinquency as a deviant psychosocial moratorium has existed for a long time, but attention is now being directed to it because it seems to be attracting too

[20] *Ibid.*, p. 6.
[21] Edward Joseph Shoben, Jr. "Toward a Concept of the Normal Personality." *The American Psychologist*, April 1957. p. 183-89.
[22] Erik H. Erikson, *op. cit.*, p. 6.

many youngsters to it from "good neighborhoods" as well as from "bad areas."

Note is taken by Erikson that during adolescence, for shorter or longer periods, youth seem to indulge in behavior exactly contrary to what is desired from them. Talcott Parsons develops this same thesis, and it will be summarized later. When this occurs, Erikson holds, there appears to be an inner anarchy which may turn in one of two directions: into a "paralysis of industry" which shows itself in apathy, lack of effort toward accomplishment, so-called laziness, and indifference to effort; or it may emerge into "pathological initiative which is crime."

Delinquents—and psychotics of certain types—Erikson implies, have one thing in common, this "paralysis of workmanship." This is described by contrast to what the normal youth or person means by "completing a job," with the feeling of having created a value or a product, as distinct from "doing a job" such as a burglary or act of destructive vandalism. Both the delinquent and the psychotic have "a mistrust in themselves, a disbelief in the possibility that they could ever complete anything of value." [23] Normal young people, as teachers and parents so well know, enjoy a "sense of workmanship" which, in itself, Erikson says, replaces the need for the thrill of destruction.

As a comment on the current scene, Erikson, in psychoanalytic terms, explains a social phenomenon:

In the astonishing increase, then, of impulsive criminal and delinquent acts perpetrated by young individuals and gangs, I see, primarily, perverse forms of what in psychoanalysis we call "turning passive into active." By this we mean that the human ego cannot stand more than a certain amount of passivity and victimization. Normally, the play of children and the games, pranks, and sports of young people, as well as imagination and intellectual pursuits, provide safety valves even as they advance capabilities and opportunities that feed into identity formation. However, where capabilities are undernourished and opportunities questionable, the lag between childish play and adult act becomes unbearable: destructive prank becomes the vehicle of initiative, which, once employed, too often—and too late—proves to possess defective brakes. [24]

A Theory of the Delinquent Ego

Fritz Redl and David Wineman, in their two volumes, *Children Who Hate* and *Controls from Within*, utilize the clinical findings of psychoanalysis, psychiatry and psychology with the broader social orientation of sociology, as they develop their theory of the delinquent

[23] *Ibid.*, p. 10-11.
[24] *Ibid.*, p. 16-17.

ego.[25] From the needs of teachers, school administrators, parents and others charged with the responsibility of "educating" or "changing" the youth to the socialized adult, these two volumes offer suggestions for the so-called normal youth as well as for the emotionally disturbed and delinquent.

Basically these men are interested in what they term "disturbances of the ego function" and the problems of control of behavior arising from such disturbances. From their own clinical findings, they attempt to supplement the social-cultural data about deviant behavior. They explain:

When we talk about the "delinquent ego" here, we have two things in mind:

1. We use the term "delinquent" in its cultural meaning—referring to any behavior which runs counter to the dominant value system within which the child's character formation takes place. . . . We mean all the attitudes which will be developed in a child who is about to drift into a "delinquent style of life."

2. As far as the "ego" side of the picture goes, we want to describe the ego in those situations in which it is bent on *defending impulse gratification at any cost.* In short, instead of performing its task of looking for a synthesis between desires, reality demands and the impact of social values, the ego is, in those moments, totally on the side of *impulsivity.* It throws all its weight into the task of making impulse gratification possible, against the outside world as well as against whatever remainders of the voice of its own conscience may be left. . . .[26]

Explanation continues that the task of the delinquent ego is to "get away with things" in an effort to "secure guilt free and anxiety free enjoyment of delinquent impulsivity. . . ."[27] This may take the form of gang participation in a deprived community area or it may take any other form which the particular personality finds available or satisfying.

Many a youngster whose behavior is occasionally delinquent has the additional problem of "duping" his own superego—or conscience —since "chunks of conscience" or the "value identified superego" remain intact.[28] How these particular youngsters develop and defend their "tough defense machinery" against their own consciences is the particular interest of Redl and Wineman. The "delinquent ego," then, is described as an "auxiliary concept" which implies "the ego

---

[25] Fritz Redl and David Wineman. *Children Who Hate* and *Controls from Within.* Glencoe, Illinois: The Free Press, 1951 and 1952.
[26] Redl and Wineman, *Children Who Hate,* p. 143-144.
[27] *Ibid.,* p. 144.
[28] *Ibid.,* p. 144.

functioning right now in a planned attempt to defend non-acceptable impulsivity." They conclude, "We have to restrict ourselves here . . . to a mere listing of the most discernible 'ego functions in the service of impulse defense.' "

Typical behavior in "the strategy of evasion" of guilt feelings are: denial to oneself of any immediate emotional gain from such behavior; the rationalizations, "We were all in on it"; "He did it first"; "But somebody else did that same thing to me before"; "I didn't use the proceeds in any way"; "But I made it up to him afterwards"; "He is a no good so-and-so himself"; "They are all against me, nobody likes me, they are always picking on me"; "I couldn't have gotten it in any other way." All of these are verbalizations which attempt to push aside inner conflict between conscience and behavior—and, it might be added, which all persons indulge in at one time or another. Redl and Wineman point up that these devices are directed toward remaining guilt free rather than warding off consequences for behavior.[29]

Delinquents, as Redl and Wineman report (and this is verified by Albert K. Cohen in his *Delinquent Boys*), need support. This they obtain by picking the wrong types of friends, the gangs they join and the mob psychology to which they submit. They incorporate into their behavior the ideals which support it, and they find these in "the slick operator," "the bad man" and the "sharpie" whom they often see portrayed in movies, television, and radio melodrama. The normal youngsters see these same dramas, but instead of making them a part of their ideals, they take out their interest by "playing like" gangsters and bandits in sort of an escape game of "cops and robbers." Delinquent youth use these antisocial examples to construct their own "self-image" while normal youngsters slough them off in imaginative play.[30]

Both delinquent and normal preadolescents and adolescents, according to these research men, enter warfare with "change agents," whether these are parents, teachers or clinicians. Strategy techniques which they utilize to escape change toward socially desirable patterns of behavior include such devices as "casing the personnel." By this procedure, youth arrive at an understanding of the whims, weaknesses, assumptions and predilections of the adults who are in charge of changing them.

Some youth, they point out, develop uncanny skills in "counter-interview" when they are under question by an adult. And, parenthetically, what adult has not found himself suddenly the questionee when

[29] *Ibid.*, p. 145-56.
[30] *Ibid.*, p. 195.

he *thought* his role was that of questioner. Moreover, when the going gets rough and the "prick of conscience" is getting painful, youth practice and develop skills in "handling people," in maneuvering the world around them, in making the most of the opportunity, in their use of tricks which would be worthy of the most legalistic mind as it provides an escape from an uncomfortable situation.

Still another, and perhaps the most frequently used technique to gain control of a situation, is provocation of anger, fury, aggression and attack in the adult even to welcoming the use of punishment to provide an escape hatch from an undesired change in behavior. Gossip concerning power personalities in charge of "education" or "change" is a frequently useful maneuver. Moreover, if hatred can be developed toward the clinician—the teacher, the administrator, the parent—then the youngster can carefully block the channels of communication and will thus escape the influence he desires to avoid.[31]

While this is a partial inventory of the longer discussion of Redl and Wineman, and while it is particularly applicable to "children who hate," they write:

. . . the ego of any child, especially the normally growing pre-adolescent and young adolescent, will at times have jobs to perform similar to those his more disturbed contemporaries have on a larger and more chronic scale. This further means that the same basic ingredients of ego defense against educational surrender and change can be observed by all teachers and parents and the technical issues of just how to go about meeting the ego that defends itself against change becomes as relevant as it is for the clinician in a treatment home.[32]

A Theory of Aggressive Behavior

Defiant behavior, out of control and directed toward immediate satisfaction, is universally recognized as a concomitant of delinquency. Because of this, a discussion of Talcott Parsons' theory of aggressive behavior is particularly pertinent though it was not written with specific relation to juvenile delinquency.

Aggression, Parsons writes, is a disposition on the part of a person or a group to act in such a way as to gain certain goals or ends through action which carries within it an intention to injure persons or groups.[33] Aggression is, of course, the emotion of anger put into action toward

[31] *Ibid.*, p. 174-91.

[32] *Ibid.*, p. 195.

[33] Talcott Parsons. "Certain Primary Sources and Patterns of Aggression in the Social Structure of the Western World." *Psychiatry*, May 1947. p. 167-81.

the destruction of whatever is proving to be the roadblock to the desires or the goals of the person. Parsons comments that the one most dangerous factor in present power relations is aggression, whether in relationships between individual persons or between groups as large as nations or blocks of nations.[34]

Parsons' theory rests on the belief that all social behavior is understandable in terms of motivation *of* persons *in* situations. Control of aggressive behavior, then, does not necessarily stem from a knowledge of causes, but also important is a knowledge of what goals or values are striving to be attained. Moreover, it is necessary to know in what directions such behavior is being turned and what motivations are being repressed or released through such action. Delinquency, as an example of aggressive behavior, should be approached by teachers, parents and community leaders, then, from these points of view if effective preventive measures are to be discovered and applied.

Immediately ruled out by Parsons as the cause of aggressive behavior is heredity as seen in "the hereditary beast of prey" who gets that way because he is born that way. Aggressive behavior, he states, arises from two basic causes: *insecurity* in interpersonal relations, and *anxiety* from feeling inadequate in performance toward standards and goals set up for the person either by powerful *others* in his own life or by society as a whole.[35]

Earliest security, Parsons reiterates, arises from the relationship between the infant or small child and his mother. When an infant senses, and then comes to understand, that his mother and other family members want him and love him, then his security within himself is on its way to achievement. This is, of course, synonymous with Erikson's concept of basic trust.

Children who because of inconsistency in the behavior of the mother, and later the father—or because of an outright lack of love—become unsure they are wanted and loved, may develop an overriding fear which expresses itself in aggressive behavior out of anger, the basis of which they may sense but which they may not always fully understand.

Apropos of Parsons' statement of the imperative of love for security, Don Peter Morris, child psychiatrist, once remarked that when children were brought to him for treatment, there was good possibility for recovery from the emotional disturbance if the child was loved by his parents. Also recovery was more difficult, but possible, for the child who knew without equivocation that he was unwanted and unloved.

[34] *Ibid.*, p. 167.
[35] *Ibid.*, p. 168.

But the child whose infancy and early years had been permeated with being accepted one day and rejected the next was indeed difficult and sometimes impossible to bring back to emotional health.

Love, to Parsons and to many other behavioral scientists, as well as religionists, is a major human dimension in all cultures. Frustration from lack of love, or ambivalence about safety within its encompassing emotional climate, is a major source of aggression.[36]

The second important component in aggression, Parsons says, is anxiety arising from a feeling of inability to meet demands of important others. This anxiety may arise either when the standards or goals for a child are set too high by parents—or teacher, or schools as a whole— or when the values, standards and goals for success in a society become unattainable.

Feelings of inadequacy are heightened, Parsons emphasizes, when the superior achievement of others is called to the attention of the non-achievers in invidious comparisons. Again, Parsons stresses the imperative of consistency and fairness of adults with children in the family, school and community. Recognition of the individual's achievement should be in line with his ability.

When there is a continued sense of failure, aggression may take either one of two directions. It may be turned against those persons who make the unachievable demands. Or, it may be directed against successful contemporaries. Herein no doubt lies the explanation of why delinquent youngsters so often vent their hatred by "picking on the good kids."

Instead of considering aggressive behavior as a pathological reaction in children, it must be recognized, Parsons insists, as an expected reaction to "strain in human relationships" at a stage of development where there is high vulnerability. Psychologists express this as strain coming at a time when there is not enough ego-strength to withstand the pressures.

In this process of inconsistency or lack of love and in continuous failure to measure up, the child or youth puts a shell around himself as a shield against continuing hurt. Once hurt, a person does not put himself in a position of being hurt again if he can help it.[37] In the area of achievement this "shell" may well be Erikson's "paralysis of industry." If a child or youth has no sense of achievement, then he avoids continuous defeat by not even trying to achieve. Here, of course, is the clue to why many youngsters in the classroom make no effort to perform even up to the level of their ability. Here, also, may be

[36] Ibid., p. 168-69.
[37] Ibid., p. 167.

the reason why some "gifted" children fall far below the expectations of parents and teachers.

Aggressive impulses become fixed, Parsons stresses, and the result is behavior without self-control, behavior in which there is a tendency to over-react in situations which call for no such reaction. Since aggressive action against family members is frowned upon and punished, and since aggression turned against self is destructively uncomfortable, there is a tendency toward displacement away from the causative sources toward a "scapegoat." If trouble has its source at home, the teacher may become the "scapegoat"; if aggression stems from a deprived slum neighborhood, then the school as a symbol of society may become the target for vandalistic wrath. This offers an explanation of why, in a culture where private property holds such value, much frustration among delinquents is displaced in destruction of this symbol of social values.

Why delinquency is more frequent among boys than girls is described in Parsons' theory. Both boys and girls in infancy and early childhood are thrown with the mother, a feminine figure, as the "significant" and controlling adult. It is she who expresses or withholds both affection and its expression in physical care. It is she who sets up the standards of behavior and achievement toward which children must strive from the beginning. Moreover, she is in the role of chief dispenser of discipline. Then school teachers, predominantly feminine, join forces with the mother and add even further strength to demands for conformity to "good behavior." [38]

Girls mature earlier than boys, Parsons believes, not only because of physical factors but also because they find no difficulty in incorporating as their ego-ideals their mothers and teachers, both feminine figures. On the other hand, boys discover very early that the one thing they cannot afford to be is a "sissy" or an effeminate male. [39]

Boys, then, come to equate tender emotions and "goodness" with the feminine, and they set out early to prove themselves masculine in opposition to the femininity under which they have developed. Basic revolt here, Parsons insists, is not against either tender emotions or goodness but against "feminine identification." When boys are in the preadolescent and adolescent periods of development, they feel impelled to exemplify physical prowess and "bad" behavior to prove their own maleness.

A valid criticism of this thesis would seem to be that if it is essential for boys to rebel against the feminine, then why should the mother

[38] *Ibid.*, p. 172.
[39] *Ibid.*, p. 171-72.

be sure her growing son knows he is loved? Moreover, one could argue that the less identification, the less need to rebel. Also the social class factor needs to be taken into account in any such argument since it is well established that the lower class male is impelled to prove his maleness even more than the middle class boy. He also has accessible the gang in which to prove his masculinity where the middle class youth does not.[40]

But to return to Parsons' thesis, "bad behavior" implies the quality of irresponsibility. Therefore, the male ideal developed by boys protesting against feminine identification is physical prowess and irresponsibility. This is further complicated because mothers often subconsciously—and sometimes consciously—admire these "masculine attributes" and give tacit approval to such behavior. This is particularly true, Parsons points out, when the developing young male has winning ways and an attractive face and figure.

Males in the United States, then, are forced to make one further transition before they finally are able to achieve "ego identity." Successful adult males in this society are men who use their minds skillfully and who depend little on their physical attributes. Moreover, their role is one of responsibility both at home, in occupations and in the community. Therefore, boys are forced to turn from their period of aggressive irresponsibility and often unsocial behavior expressed through physical acts of prowess or daring, to the role of maturity which demands intellectual competence and responsibility, as well as use of responsive positive emotions in relationships.[41]

Erikson's *psychosocial moratorium* coincides in part, at least, with the "bad boy" period of Parsons and as a transitional adaptive process between childhood and maturity. Within this theory one can see the possible explanation of delinquency among middle class youth who are so much under the domination of feminine figures. However, it should be stressed that pressure for conformity with middle class standards is highly significant in delinquency among working class children, while in the middle class itself the pressure is often greater on the achievement of high goals of success.[42] Both of these pressures on children and youth in both socioeconomic groups may well lead to the "revolt toward maleness" which may end in loss of self-control

[40] Informal and unpublished critique by Robert L. Sutherland.

[41] Parsons, *op. cit.*, p. 172.

[42] Parsons' article carries his analysis of aggression not only through kinship, but to problems of status through occupational demands, through the impact of the fundamental processes of dynamic change, and into an analysis of the institutional structures through which aggression is channeled such as delinquency, crime, prejudice and intolerance.

in behavior. Again, the revulsion against "tender emotions" not only may be a possible explanation of "unfeeling behavior" of working class children and gang delinquents, but of everyday noted "unfeeling behavior" of so-called normal middle class youth.

"Anomie" or Normless Behavior

Values, as Parsons and others stress, are important directional guides for behavior. Robert K. Merton, building upon the original theory of Emile Durkheim, the French sociologist, describes the impact of valuelessness upon the behavior of persons. Especially, he applies this concept to juvenile delinquency.[43]

The state of being without values or norms is given the designation of *anomie* by both Durkheim and Merton. *Anomie* has its Greek roots in the word, *nomos*, or law or norm. Durkheim's term in French means without law or without norms. While his primary interest was in the consequences of *anomie,* Merton discussed it from the point of view of lack of opportunity to achieve cultural values because of "the underlying social organization." [44]

Cultural values, to Merton, mean an organized set of norms which is recognized and accepted by members of a designated group. On the other hand, social structure means an organized set of social relationships in which members of designated groups are involved.

According to Merton, deviant behavior, such as delinquency, does not necessarily arise from "impulses of individuals breaking through social controls," but it may well come about because of "socially induced deviations—deviations which the culture and the social organization conjoin to produce. . . ." [45]

Merton points out that members in this society are expected to achieve success and to strive for it. All members of all classes do not accept this value emphasis, Merton indicates, primarily because the possibility of attainment of success is "imperfectly integrated" into the social structure. Values (or social norms), according to this theory, do not develop in persons unless there is some possibility of gaining at least some of these ends. Without any access to achievement, there is no establishment of goals toward which to work.[46]

[43] Robert K. Merton. *New Perspectives for Research on Juvenile Delinquency,* Helen L. Witmer and Ruth Kotinsky, editors. p. 24-50.
[44] For the development of the theory of *anomie,* see Robert K. Merton, *Social Theory and Social Structure,* Glencoe, Illinois: The Free Press, 1949.
[45] Merton, *New Perspectives,* p. 29.
[46] *Ibid.,* p. 29.

Personalities operating without norms to guide behavior, Harry Estill Moore has indicated, make the sociological concept of *anomie* and the psychological concept of *psychopathic* personality closely akin, and, in turn, offer a sociological explanation for a psychological phenomenon.

Because there is no value system in personalities or groups does not mean there is no desire to obtain at least the surface symbols of values of the predominant cultural structure. Hence, delinquent or criminal behavior often is directed toward the acquisition of such symbols of success as automobiles stolen rather than purchased, jewels and clothes obtained through burglary or bought with the proceeds of burglary, and position attained by being a "slick operator" rather than achieved by being a productive person.

Merton stresses the necessity for a distinction between the sociological and psychological definitions of normal behavior and the statistical count which is considered "the norm" when in truth it is more accurately the mode or behavior of the majority. Merton states, ". . . the sociologist regards those behaviors as normal that do not make for certain kinds of instability in the social system, in precisely the same way as the psychologist regards those as normal which do not make for certain kinds of instability in the individual." [47] Therefore, he points out, one cannot apply relative frequency or absolute standards as determining factors in delinquent or other deviant behavior. But where there is a progressive breakdown of values, then deviant behavior arises.

Where there is *anomie*—and the "loss of orientation on the part of a substantial number of members of the group" toward the norms of the majority—then a new set of norms or values may have to be developed within the over-all social organization. From the development of a new set of values—negative or positive—may come "a shift from relative breakdown and social isolation, which is found intolerable, to reintegration in a new group." [48] Youngsters who find themselves precluded from obtaining at least the material symbols of values and feel themselves isolates among other isolates, may well reintegrate their value system through the formation of the delinquent gang with its own socially negative value structure. *Anomie*, then, no longer exists because there are developed values which may be attained in the social organization of the gang in a slum community.

Merton warns that in new approaches to research in delinquency, there must not be too much thinking and research about:

[47] *Ibid.*, p. 34.
[48] *Ibid.*, p. 40.

. . . the particular individual in his local setting as though the remote total structure had no bearing on him unless we happened to detect it by direct inquiry of him. Looking at the larger social structure . . . gives clues to pressures on intervening social units in which the individual does in fact live out his life, in which he is located, but which are continually changing their composition and their character, both culturally and socially. I see it as the office of the field of sociology primarily to attempt to import these considerations into the study of deviant behavior just as I would see the same kind of elaboration as the office of a psychologist dealing with the structure and dynamics of the psyche.[49]

It might be added that both sociological and psychological examination of the problems of delinquency and its prevention are essential supplements one to the other if useful tools for curative and preventive action are to be obtained by parents and teachers, law enforcement officers, school officials, and other community leaders.

The Theory of Differential Association

Edwin H. Sutherland, noted criminologist, offered a formula for describing social situations out of which criminals are produced or where education of the young is toward delinquent behavior.

Criminology, Sutherland explained, is a body of knowledge which concerns itself with making laws to govern behavior, with breaking of these laws, and the reaction of persons toward law breaking. Certain acts become, therefore, defined as criminal even as others are recognized as delinquent.[50]

An adequate explanation of the origin of criminal or delinquent behavior, Sutherland believed, does not exist unless it applies to "rich and poor alike, and to the emotionally stable or unstable." Moreover, it must apply directly to criminal or delinquent behavior—not to human behavior in general. The life history of the delinquent or criminal has to be taken into account rather than a single act if an adequate explanation of even a single act is to be obtained. Therefore, he offered what he called "a genetic theory" of criminality. This he stated in a series of propositions:

Criminal behavior is learned. Persons not trained in crime do not invent criminal behavior.

Criminal behavior, like any other behavior, is learned in interaction

---

[49] *Ibid.*, p. 42-43.
[50] Edwin H. Sutherland. *Principles of Criminology.* Fourth edition. Philadelphia: J. B. Lippincott Company, 1947. p. 1.

with other people through communication, both verbal and through gestures.
The principal part of the learning of a criminal is accomplished in his intimate and personal groups—family, play group, school, etc. Newspapers, radio, television, and the like play a relatively minor role in such learning.

When criminal behavior is learned, it includes techniques, skills, and abilities which are applied to committing crime. Also certain motivations, drives, rationalizations, and attitudes are learned toward delinquent behavior.

A person becomes a criminal or delinquent where there is an excess of definitions in his primary group which are in favor of law violation as opposed to definitions in favor of abiding by the law.

Differential association—with law abiders or law breakers—may vary in frequency, duration, priority, and intensity.

The process of learning criminal behavior involves all the mechanisms that are involved in any other type of learning.

While criminal or delinquent behavior is an expression of general needs and values, it is not explainable by these because non-criminal behavior is also an expression of needs and values.[51]

To Edwin H. Sutherland, as is evident, crime and delinquency are rooted in and are expressions of social organization. He emphasized that all communities are organized both for criminal and anti-criminal behavior. Exposure, both in duration and strength, is the important factor as to whether one becomes delinquent or remains law abiding.[52]

Psychiatrists, psychologists and many sociologists do not accept this statement of the cause of delinquency since it does not take into account complexity of personalities and problems of conflict within personalities. Also, it does not explain why many of the "exposed" do not "learn" delinquent behavior, while some who are "underexposed" to such learning do indulge in delinquent acts. As Marshall B. Clinard points out, "Obviously, as stated by Sutherland, the theory does not adequately recognize motivations and the situation as a part of the learning process." Other criticisms stress that delinquent behavior cannot be explained aside from personality traits and attitudes. Donald R. Cressy insists that delinquency needs to be studied from basic learning theory rather than from Edwin Sutherland's mathematical ratio of criminal to noncriminal association.[53]

[51] These are paraphrased from Sutherland's listing, *ibid.*, p. 6-7.

[52] *Ibid.*, p. 8-9.

[53] See these and other critical issues in delinquency and criminology in *Review of Sociology,* Joseph B. Gittler, editor, New York: John Wiley and Sons, 1957. p. 477.

A Theory of Cultural Transmission

Albert K. Cohen in *Delinquent Boys* states that the differential theory of Sutherland harks back to the earlier statement of cultural transmission of delinquent behavior as presented by Clifford R. Shaw and Henry D. McKay in 1921 and restated in 1942.[54]

No doubt exists, Shaw and McKay write, that there is a direct relationship existing between delinquency and the socioeconomic factors in local communities. Differential rates of delinquency have their roots in "the dynamic life of the community." This "dynamic life" in delinquency areas includes differences in social values, norms and attitudes as well as poverty and insufficiency in material goods. Delinquency, in certain urban areas, has become a tradition in itself. These authors believe:

This tradition is manifested in many different ways. It becomes meaningful to the child through the conduct, speech, gestures, and attitudes of persons with whom he has contact. Of particular importance is the child's intimate association with predatory gangs or other forms of delinquent and criminal organization.

. . . In cases of group delinquency it may be said, therefore, that from the point of view of the delinquent's immediate social world he is not necessarily disorganized, maladjusted or antisocial. Within the limits of his social world and in terms of its norms and expectations he may be a highly organized and well adjusted person.[55]

In low income areas, these authors stress, where there is both great deprivation and frustration, where there has been a succession of immigrant and migrant groups, where there has been the widest variation in cultural traditions and institutions, where there is a great gap between what people have come to want out of the social values of the over-all culture and what they can get from their own limited environment, crime and delinquency develop as a way of life.

Again, these scholars note that delinquent traditions grow up under the impetus of the belief that through these behaviors will come improved economic and social status. Illegal rackets have brought wealth to many. Material goods do bring a measure of status. Men have acquired political prominence through antisocial channels. Children and youth do take over the traditional behavior which appears to assure them success, wealth and position.[56]

[54] Clifford R. Shaw and Henry D. McKay. *Juvenile Delinquency in Urban Areas*. Chicago: The University of Chicago Press, 1942. Copyright, 1942, by the University of Chicago.

[55] *Ibid.*, p. 436.

[56] *Ibid.*, p. 439-40.

However, as Shaw and McKay point out, the dominant tradition of cities and of communities is, on the whole, conventional. Most persons even in underprivileged areas pursue law abiding careers. This does not deny the power of tradition of delinquency and crime to attract followers, but it does point to the reason the majority do not become delinquent or criminal even in acutely deprived areas. Shaw and McKay state:

Individual and personality differences as well as differences in family relationships and in contacts with other institutions and groups, no doubt influence greatly his acceptance or rejection of opportunities to engage in delinquent activities. It may be said, however, that if the delinquency traditions were not present and the boys were not thus exposed to it, a preponderance of those who become delinquent in low-income areas would find their satisfactions in activities other than delinquency.[57]

The Delinquent Subculture* ✓

Albert K. Cohen presents a near case study illustrating in part the blending of the theory of cultural transmission, the theory of *anomie*, and others previously discussed *plus* his own contribution of the concept of the delinquent subculture within the larger social structure. Cohen remarks that a fascinating aspect of social process is how persons move from group to group and how there is a realignment within groups in an unconscious quest for a socially favorable milieu in which to resolve problems of personal adjustment.[58]

In describing the development of delinquent gangs, Cohen calls attention to models for behavior in different milieu, and these models are always in the process of interaction. From these interactions emerge cultural innovations even in the face of pressures for conformity. He writes:

The crucial condition for the emergence of new cultural forms is the existence, *in effective interaction with one another, of a number of actors with similar problems of adjustment.* These may be entire membership of a group or only certain members, similarly circumscribed, within the group.[59]

* For other treatments of the gang phenomenon, see: Frederic M. Thrasher, *The Gang* (2nd rev. ed.), Chicago: The University of Chicago Press, 1936; William Foote White, *Street Corner Society* (2nd ed.), Chicago: The University of Chicago Press, 1955; and Herbert A. Bloch and Arthur Niederhoffer, *The Gang: A Study of Adolescent Behavior*, New York: Philosophical Library, 1958.

[57] *Ibid.*, p. 440-41.

[58] Albert K. Cohen. *Delinquent Boys.* Glencoe, Ill.: The Free Press, 1955. p. 58.

[59] *Ibid.*, p. 59.

Possible solutions for problems may not appear to be through acceptable behavior, but they may appeal more than "the already validated and accepted institutionalized solutions." However, the new way of behaving would not be a possible adjustment unless it were followed by others so that the person with the problem is not alone in his new way of behaving. If others with common problems are contemplating or indulging in the proposed behavior, and this is determined by subtle communication between those of like problems, then these maladjusted will join up and elaborate on the behavior which appears to be mutually acceptable.[60] Cohen succinctly remarks that, "Converting the other is a part of the process of converting oneself."[61]

Mob or gang action sets up its own "positive morality" or value structure to justify its conduct with a rapid transition into behavior according to new "group standards" with the emergence of a distinctive subculture.[62]

This is what occurs, according to Cohen, when the problem of achieving status and recognition from others is blocked by whatever forces, be they cultural, environmental, broadly social. Problems of status are recognized as of critical importance to youth. When youngsters find it impossible to achieve status according to broader based social standards, then they turn to the development of "characteristics they do possess and the kinds of conduct of which they are capable. . . ."[63]

The new values which emerge may be diametrically opposed to the larger cultural structure. Actual and overt hostility may be expressed toward the *out* group which has kept the new *in* group from sharing in status and accord. Cohen points out that the new group, the gang, cannot exist in isolation any more than the youngsters within the gang can stand being isolates. The gang must get its needs satisfied from the prevailing culture, and in the underworld this is known as "the fix."

Acquisition of status in the new group is, of necessity, achieved at the cost of loss of status in the other group. Hostile and contemptuous images of the outside group are built up in the new group, and behavior is indulged in simply because "it is disreputable in the eyes of the out group."[64]

Delinquent subcultures are more often found in working class groups, Cohen states. And these have arisen because personal problems of defeat and inadequacy have become so intense and demanding that a new group solution is the only possible solution. If the

[60] *Ibid.*, p. 59-60. [61] *Ibid.*, p. 61. [62] *Ibid.*, p. 65. [63] *Ibid.*, p. 66. [64] *Ibid.*, p. 68.

solution remains personal-social, then the resolution will probably be "neurotic" or "psychotic."

Problems of adjustment of boys from working class homes have much in common. Socialization in the working class is easy going, while in the middle class little is left to chance. An appropriate comment was recently made by Gardner Murphy of the Menninger Foundation. Murphy stated a growing conviction that neighborhoods where youngsters grow up depending upon their peer group instead of upon their parents "have a much higher incidence of conscienceless" behavior.[65]

Distinctions between middle class and working class groups from the point of view of values shed real light on why youngsters from the latter find themselves ill equipped to gain status through achievement of values of the former.

The middle class is distinguished by regarding ambition as a virtue and lack of it, a serious defect. Goals are long term and require "worldly asceticism" and readiness to postpone immediate temptations for future satisfactions. Responsibility is individual, and reliance and resourcefulness are considered essentials. Skills have to be developed in order that there may be tangible achievements through outstanding performances either in the scholastic, the athletic or the artistic areas. Forethought, conscious planning, and budgeting of time are considered of high value. Manners, courtesy, charm and other skills in relationships are the basis for "selling" of self to others. Aggression is controlled, and violence and physical combat are frowned upon. Recreation has to be such that it is considered "wholesome," "constructive," and not a "waste of time." Property must be respected. To achieve status and success, Cohen states, these are the ground rules of the prevailing culture in the United States.[66]

Contrasted to these are the working class norms. Ambition and aspirations toward jobs are below those of the middle class. A "swell job" is not necessarily considered a step toward economic mobility. "Advancement" and "promotion" are not in the vocabulary of the working class. "Planning" and "foresight" are outside the range of values. The "pinch of the present" is far more demanding than "the promise of the future." A "run of good luck" is to furnish the wherewithal to buy what is wanted, not the basis of a savings account. "Pay off" is considered an immediate need, not eventual upgrading. The "ethic of responsibility" for the down-and-out in the family is im-

---

[65] Fall of 1957.
[66] Cohen, *op. cit.*, p. 89-91.

perative to the extent that one branch of the family will spend all it has for another in need. And the "law of reciprocity" holds, in that the same is expected in return in times of stress. One is honest with particular persons, not honest in general. Persons in this socio-economic group feel more at home in their own families and in the immediate neighborhood, and are ill at ease in secondary social contacts so prevalent in the middle class. Emotions appear to be released more spontaneously and there is freer expression of aggression with no hesitancy to fight. Little attempt is made to cultivate polish, sophistication, "fluency," "appearance" and "personality" considered so necessary in the middle class world.[67]

Warning must be given, of course, that neither middle class nor working class families adhere strictly to these definitions. In fact, with the rapid upward mobility in the United States, characteristics herein described are found interchanged in all groups in the culture. But from the point of view of stress in adjustment of adolescent boys, the statement of differences is essential to Cohen's theory.

Cohen says that the delinquent subculture is a solution to the problems of status and success for the male rather than for the female.[68] Girls find success in relationships with boys within their own status group as well as outside. Popularity, pulchritude, charm and clothes are central to feminine success.

Even though girls may succeed as students, in a career or in any other medium, success to them is not complete without achievement in the "symbolic relationship of woman attractive to man." [69]

Male delinquency is versatile. Female delinquency is usually specialized in sex or in obtaining those goods which are necessary to become attractive to the other sex. Female delinquency is harder to detect, and this may well be why it is less often counted to the extreme difference in delinquency rates between boys and girls.

The final question, then, is who are the boys who join the subculture of the gang? Cohen explains the obvious that personality is complex in its needs, roles, activities, aspirations and problems. The gang, he believes, is the one avenue for furnishing satisfactory answers for many different youth with many different problems in the working class. To it come boys from ethnic groups which are without privilege or opportunity. To the gang will gravitate those who are afraid they will be beaten up by gangs in their own neighborhoods.

[67] *Ibid.*, p. 94-97.
[68] *Ibid.*, p. 143.
[69] *Ibid.*, p. 142.

To belong is protection. Others join from a sense of guilt, or hostility, of flight from anxiety. However, by far the "common core" come with a motivation widely shared by others—the need for achievement and success by *some* standard.[70] While it must be remembered the psychiatric explanation of delinquency is a valid one in explaining the behavior of particular individuals, it tends to leave out "cultural support and legitimation of particular solutions" to problems which are social and cultural in origin.

Cohen states briefly that middle class delinquency exists but is relatively rare; possibly because the families of these youth serve as a "cushion against apprehension" but mostly because their status problems are less acute and are not in conflict with the over-all value structure of the culture. Whatever may be the etiology of problems of middle class delinquency, Cohen holds, it should not be forgotten that basically it also includes problems of adjustment at a different level and with a somewhat different content than those problems of lower class youth which seek their solution in delinquent gangs.[71]

Delinquency in Suburbia

Bertram M. Beck has developed a theory as current as community development in suburban areas which is worthy of note.[72] Basing his discussion on a recent book by Bernard Lander,[73] he points out that the delinquent in the suburb, as the migrant in the slums, comes about because of intergroup conflict which works against social conformity. Each family moves into the new area as a unit, without ties to any other family and without antecedents of its own. Tradition is entirely lacking, and anonymity of family groups is almost complete until a new set of associations is built up with other anonymous families.

Community organization and services are also lacking. Churches are new or nonexistent. The community trading center has to develop its friendliness as families come to know one another, and the huge supermarkets are a far cry from the intimacy of the corner drugstore and the family-run grocery or market.

Youth find little support from the adults in such communities, and they also find little cohesiveness in youth groups which are brought

[70] *Ibid.*, p. 151.

[71] *Ibid.*, p. 161.

[72] Bertram M. Beck. "The School and Delinquency Control." *The Annals of the American Academy of Political and Social Science*, November 1955, p. 66.

[73] Bernard Lander. *Toward an Understanding of Juvenile Delinquency.* New York: Columbia University Press, 1954.

together on a heterogeneous basis. The school is the sole center for total community organization since it serves all the children of all families, and is a common meeting ground for adults as well as their children.

Suburbs, to avoid the development of delinquent behavior among children and youth without the ordinary social controls of a neighborhood of friends, acquaintances and relatives, need more than any other one agent "a strong and courageous school administrator." The administrator and his staff have a tremendous obligation to make the school the focal point for community integration, for an organized source of community action, for the establishment of acceptable traditions of behavior, and for concerted community action to meet the needs of youth and children.[74]

Schools, Beck believes, have the responsibility to create the moral, social and ethical climate within these new agglomerations of houses so that community controls will be developed to protect the youth of suburbia against delinquency and related ills.[75]

[74] For studies of the role of school administrators as community leaders, see Harry Estill Moore, *Nine Help Themselves*, Austin, Texas: Southwestern Cooperative Program in Educational Administration, The University of Texas, 1955.

[75] Beck, *op. cit.*, p. 67.

CHAPTER 5

The Schools and the Problems of Juvenile Delinquents

SAMUEL MILLER BROWNELL, former commissioner for the United States Office of Education and now superintendent of schools in Detroit, Michigan, has written that the existence of juvenile delinquency proves in a broad sense that education has not been fully successful. He states that, even in combination, the institutions of education for children—the home, school and church with other community groups—have not been able to prevent more and more youth from becoming delinquent.[1]

Harrison E. Salisbury, journalist, in his series of articles on "The Shook-Up Generation," in the *New York Times,* writes:

No New Yorker needs to be told that it is in the city's schools the problem of "shook-up" adolescents reaches a stormy climax. Ever since the novel and film *Blackboard Jungle,* New Yorkers have been increasingly aware of the impact of teen-age violence on the educational system. In recent weeks, there has been a new series of tragic incidents.[2]

And from another educator of note comes this statement:

With the rise in juvenile delinquency, the medicine men are once again prescribing their favorite panacea. For prevention and cure of delinquency, we are advised to "get tough," "go back to the woodshed," "apply the nightstick". . . . Naturally, the advocates of the return to the woodshed are among the severest critics of modern programs of education. Their editorial spokesmen satirically deride "the bleeding hearts who say education is the answer". . . .[3]

Another comment is worthy of attention since it comes from Jessie

[1] Samuel Miller Brownell. "Delinquency—An Important Problem in Education." *School Life,* January 1954. p. 52-53.

[2] Harrison E. Salisbury. Reprint from *The New York Times,* March 23-30, 1958. p. 8.

[3] William Van Til. "Combating Juvenile Delinquency Through Schools." *Educational Leadership,* March 1956. p. 362-63.

C. Binford, social worker at Hull House in Chicago for more than 30 years:

The sad fact is that some of our Juvenile Court Judges and many educators agree . . . that the only solution to juvenile delinquency is work for our children.

It does not seem to occur to these that we owe our children an education —which is all too little now—and that we must adapt our curriculum to the needs of children—so that they will *want* to remain in school at least until they are 16 years of age. . . .[4]

In light of available facts, it may be well to state as have Brownell, the educator, and Salisbury, the journalist, that between 95 and 98 percent of school-age children are normal personalities, reasonably healthy, and law abiding. Of the under five percent who express their deviation in delinquency, 95 percent of the seventeen-year-olds, 85 percent of the sixteen-year-olds, and 50 percent of the fifteen-year-olds are not in school. In fact, approximately 61 percent of the delinquents between the ages of eight and seventeen years are out of school.[5]

Delinquency, Brownell continues, is related to public schools in three ways: Schools may produce delinquency. Schools may help prevent delinquency. Schools may help deal with delinquents through curriculum and program of activities.[6]

The Schools as Producers of Behavior Problems

The most startling of these three statements, is that the school may contribute to the development of delinquency through offering frustrating experiences, by not maintaining interest, by not releasing tensions built up in other relationships, and by not developing a feeling of satisfaction among youngsters which will keep them from, or move them out of, delinquent behavior.[7]

As factors which enter into the failure of schools to hold children or which may contribute to delinquency, Brownell cites poor preparation of teachers in detection of special needs of children; lack of time for teachers to really know the children they teach; and failure of the

[4] Letter, May 3, 1956. (Letters quoted throughout this section were answers to a request addressed by the author to members of the Discussion Group 57, Tenth Annual Conference of the Association for Supervision and Curriculum Development, Chicago, Illinois, 1955.)

[5] Brownell, *op. cit.*, p. 52.

[6] *Ibid.*, p. 52.

[7] *Ibid.*, p. 52.

schools to provide teachers with special assistance they require in dealing with severe behavior problems. [8]

Adding strength to the Brownell evaluation is a letter from a mother of teen-age youth and a former director of the Illinois Parent-Teacher Association. She explains:

> As I listen to my teenagers and their friends speaking about the teachers, I feel the poor caliber of some of our teachers contributes more to delinquency than they realize through mass punishments, criticism of the slow child openly in classrooms, and complaining of the overwork of all teachers. I realize we need more teachers, but I am also sure we need better trained teachers. We also need more counseling in our local high schools, perhaps even guidance clinics. But let us get some real counselors who are willing to listen to boys and girls. . . .[9]

Howard W. Lane, in remarks made on a symposium of the American Orthopsychiatric Association in 1956, said he had "made a little survey out on Long Island to see what it means to a school child to live in the suburbs." He discovered "five important hazards to a child." The most serious, he indicates, is to be a slow reader. The second is to be a boy, to whom many more symptoms of poor mental health were attributed than to girls. Girls, he says, mature earlier and are easier to have around. The third hazard is to be left-handed, and he states there is no doubt that "the attention and the little discriminations a 'lefty' experiences chip away at mental health." He admits reluctance to list two more "little hazards" but goes on to say these are to have mother *away from home* a good deal and to have father *at home* a good deal![10] Lane is making the plea that schools must be built and organized to accommodate childlike behavior, and that there are too few places, including homes, which are now available for children to be and to act like children.

William C. Kvaraceus, in his *Juvenile Delinquency and the School*,[11] describes the Passaic, New Jersey, child welfare experiment in co-operative action among the school system, the police department and other agencies dealing with children. He quotes [12] Arthur C. Johnson as having remarked that the delinquent child may be an inescapable headache for the schools, but the schools may be an even greater head-

[8] *Ibid.*, p. 53.

[9] Letter from Mrs. Raymond H. Thompson, March 16, 1956.

[10] Howard Lane. "Educational Aspects of Prevention." *American Journal of Orthopsychiatry*, April 1957. p. 246-51. Excerpts from mimeographed reprint, p. 4-5.

[11] William C. Kvaraceus. *Juvenile Delinquency and the School.* New York: World Book Company, 1945.

[12] *Ibid.*, p. 156.

ache for the deviant child! Kvaraceus believes that the salutary effects of the school for the delinquent are too often taken for granted. He states that "much of the school data points to a multiplicity of un-wholesome, unsatisfactory, unhappy, and frustrating situations in which delinquents are enmeshed. Some schools appear to furnish experiences which are predisposing to aggressive behavior." [13]

Among these experiences is retardation, which is open acknowledgment of failure to achieve. Kvaraceus states that one great difference between the general youth population in school and the delinquent is the "rejection and condemnation" of the delinquent because he so often fails to be promoted from grade to grade.[14] Habits of failure and feelings of inferiority are characteristic of delinquency, Kvaraceus continues, and he believes it is no wonder these youth resort to rebellion and flight from the classroom. Truancy and vandalism, he indicates, are more than likely direct protests against frustrating and defeating experiences in school.[15]

In addition, delinquents themselves cited as reasons for dislike of school: clothes which were not as good as those of the other children; made fun of by the teacher; inability to get along "with the crowd"; in class with "a lot of dumb clucks"; and discipline for tardiness.[16]

Finally, in a discussion session on juvenile delinquency at the Tenth Annual Conference of the Association for Supervision and Curriculum Development in 1955, a group of school administrators, teachers, social workers, and others added several items to this list of negative forces in the schools. These were: textbooks often too difficult for use or understanding by children from underprivileged families and areas; the difficult problem of keeping in school those children whose parents have no interest in school attendance; the stereotyped subject matter curriculum of many high schools; teachers who are excessively permissive or excessively rigid in control or who are inconsistent in discipline; and careless gossip among teachers about children who have been in trouble or whose families are in difficulty.[17]

Donald H. Goff, chief, Bureau of Classification and Education, Department of Institutions and Agencies for the State of New Jersey, adds a different dimension to the discussion of the role of schools in creating negative reactions in children. He is primarily concerned with

---

[13] *Ibid.*, p. 135.
[14] *Ibid.*, p. 140.
[15] *Ibid.*, p. 144.
[16] Quoted by Kvaraceus, *ibid.*, p. 50.
[17] Mimeographed notes, Discussion Group 57, *op. cit.*, p. 2.

"the importance in the whole delinquency problem . . . of fundamental attitudes of youngsters toward behavior norms." If there were one clearly defined set of behavior norms, Goff indicates, the whole problem would be simplified. However, great heterogeneity of population and the impersonality and high mobility of urban living tend to bring about wide differences in what is considered acceptable behavior.

Schools, Goff believes, attempt to teach a single standard of normative values which brings about a rigidity in what is accepted as normal behavior by children. This creates confusion, because many children or youth are confronted with unreal behavior standards as far as their home and neighborhood experiences have taught them.[18] Merton would indicate the result is *anomie* or normlessness.

Harry Estill Moore has discussed this at some length when he writes:

There is, it seems, a double code of morality; one for natives and one for the school people. Just here, it may be speculated, may be a fertile source of rejection of the teacher as "impractical" by youth and adults. Having imposed an abnormal behavior code on the teachers, the community then brands them as abnormal, and views them with suspicion, relegating them to the role of "stranger." [19]

Moore goes on to quote Willard Waller as having said school tends to become "a museum of virtue," and then he adds, "implying that like other museums what is found there belongs to another world, not the world in which normal beings manage their affairs." [20]

Goff verifies this point of view when he writes that delinquents in training schools seem to hold a stereotype of "schoolmarm" tied in with the rigidity of middle class behavior norms as imposed in school. Goff concludes that the schools are confronted with the problem of consensus "in order to allow for group living," but that this consensus can best be reached on the level of interpersonal relations grounded in the principle of the dignity and worth of each human being rather than focusing upon one act or another as "wrong" or "right" behavior.

In fact, Goff would like to see a rigid subject-centered high school experiment with the development of attitudes toward the basic value and worth of human beings as compared with a similar attempt on the part of a school with a modified subject-centered program where interest in the human personality is the core of the whole curriculum.[21]

[18] Goff, letter, May 4, 1956.

[19] Harry Estill Moore. *Nine Help Themselves.* Austin, Texas: Southwestern Cooperative Program in Educational Administration, The University of Texas, 1955. p. 61.

[20] *Ibid.*, p. 62.

[21] Goff, letter, *op. cit.*

Cohen, it appears from his theory of the delinquent subculture, would agree with Goff that conflict between standards *of* school and standards of youth *attending* school are of major importance both in the definition of what is a delinquent act and in the instigation of behavior which may become delinquent.

Delinquents in School

Albert Reiss, Jr., in a study of "Social Correlates of Psychological Types of Delinquency,"[22] writes that delinquent behavior is a function of the nature and strength of both personal internal controls and social controls. He states:

A major institution of the community exercising social control over the child is the school. At the same time, the school affects the formation of personal controls insofar as its personnel represent acceptable models of authority and provide rational guides for behavior. Among adolescents the school may often be supplemented by or rejected as a control institution for the work institutions of the community or the adolescent peer culture.[23]

Reiss distinguishes between three types of delinquents: (a) Those with relative personality integration, or the first "Tom" of Robert L. Sutherland's discussion, whose only problem was the conflict of his social group with the dominant culture pattern. (b) The delinquent with weak ego controls; or as Marie Jahoda would indicate, one whose reality orientation is inadequate; or, again, as Erik Erikson would describe him as a victim of ego diffusion, is Reiss' second group. (c) The third designation is the delinquent with weak superego or value controls, or the victim of *anomie* as Merton would designate him.

Of these three, it is the delinquent with relatively high integration who more often achieves the level of high school, and Reiss found 53 percent of those in his study had gone to or completed high school.

Only 39 percent of those with defective value structure or weak superego achieved high school status; and 33 percent who reached high school level were those in the weak ego group. Also the latter group were more often retarded than those with defective superego, and both of these groups were more retarded than the integrated youth.

Reiss found that the relatively strong personalities among the delinquents were better students than either of the other two groups. Their deportment in the classroom was superior and their truancy rate was less. Reiss adds that youth with faulty value structures, or

[22] Albert Reiss, Jr. "Social Correlates of Psychological Types of Delinquency." *American Sociological Review*, December 1952. p. 710-18.

[23] *Ibid.*, p. 11.

the victims of *anomie,* were more often found in gangs than either the integrated or weak ego delinquents, and that those of weak ego controls were insecure with low self-esteem and indulged in highly aggressive and hostile behavior.[24]

Bertram M. Beck offers suggestions to public school teachers when he points out there are problems of delinquency with which teachers cannot and should not attempt to cope. He insists work with delinquents in school has to be diagnostic and not on the basis of lumping "delinquency" into a single category as one would a disease such as diphtheria with its specific cause and cure.[25]

No cohesive typing of delinquency has been worked out, Beck stresses, but certain studies have been made which should prove helpful to teachers and school administrators in diagnosis of delinquents in terms of whether they may be successfully integrated into the classroom situation, whether they may be assisted by counseling and guidance services within the schools, whether they should be referred to psychiatric and psychological clinics, or whether, for the protection of everyone concerned, they should be sent to law enforcement authorities. Interestingly enough, Beck uses the Jenkins-Hewitt study, discussed in Chapter 4 of this booklet, for his diagnostic instrument.

School and the Social Delinquent

Beck points out in his article that the "social delinquent" as he would describe the integrated delinquent of Reiss, will and can respond to a school curriculum especially designed to enrich his experiences, and such a curriculum serves as a vital supplement in cases of neighborhood and family deprivation. A telling example of this approach is described by Salisbury [26] in the article, "Operation More." Sidney I. Lipsyte is principal of an "exceptional 600" school in Brooklyn. Mrs. Cecile Sands, a member of the Board of Education, insisted that a school especially designed for difficult behavior problems would succeed if it had additional appropriations to get what it really needed in such areas as guidance, psychiatric aid, and after-school programs. Salisbury remarks that "nothing is provided for the school that any prudent school board would not provide in the first place" for all schools.

Youngsters who normally would be turned out of school at 3:00 stay

[24] *Ibid.,* p. 716-18.
[25] Beck, "The School and Delinquency Control," p. 60-61.
[26] Salisbury, "The Shook-Up Generation," p. 10.

under supervision until 5:00 in the afternoon. Average after-school attendance runs between 30 and 40 boys, and these are the "bad boys" of gangs who are unacceptable to neighborhood community centers. Lipsyte says of his school, "Too often it is pictured as a holding operation. We see it as a therapeutic operation. Most of our boys are the better for coming to us. . . ." He believes about 90 percent of his boys become useful citizens, and he refuses to judge their behavior by the standards of the middle class world.[27]

All-day schools, Beck indicates, are of tremendous importance to the social delinquent since the school furnishes him a "protected environment" for his own safety as well as for his development. Expert, male supervision, he points out, is an imperative. Moreover, the school and the school board have to be ready to accept disruption, property damage, and "different" behavior—as Lipsyte of "Operation More" does.

Curriculum, Beck continues, has to meet cultural differences and class differences. Teachers do have to teach values of the larger society —as Goff indicated with his insistence on the value of human personality—but they do not have to impose middle class behavior standards. Beck also believes that the best teachers of social delinquents are men who have grown up in the neighborhood. He advocates recruitment of teachers from high schools in the gang areas with scholarships as incentives for the able to go to college and train as teachers for youth with social inequities in their lives such as they, themselves, have experienced. In addition, he indicates, teachers in these schools should be paid a premium since this type of teaching takes dedication to a cause as well as to a profession.[28]

Early detection of social delinquents, according to Beck, comes from among those who are truant and from among those who are retarded in reading. Schools in areas of high delinquency require an extra supply of teachers of remedial reading plus qualified social workers, psychologists and psychiatrists. He also believes when truancy occurs among too many too frequently, the curriculum should be changed forthwith. Schools can do little for the social delinquent, Beck stresses, without these resources and without work with parents who are not too concerned whether their children remain in school or not.[29]

Detroit Public Schools tried an experiment a number of years ago

[27] *Ibid.*, p. 10.
[28] Beck, *op. cit.*, p. 62.
[29] *Ibid.*, p. 63.

which may prove of interest to schools located near colleges and universities. This was part of a larger attempt directed by Paul E. Johnson under the over-all title, "The Detroit School and Community Pilot Project for Reducing Delinquent Behavior " Among other important phases of this program was the unique attempt to bring remedial assistance to larger numbers of children in one of the schools in which intensive effort was being made to assist youngsters with problems. The College of Education of Wayne University made available nine student teachers who served as special tutors for children with special academic difficulties in the fifth and sixth grades. One person of this group worked with children from the first through the fourth grade. Tutorial aid was given in improving handwriting, in developing vocabulary as well as reading ability, and in arithmetic. Listed as benefits of this "100-hour program" of special help were improvement in basic skills in reading, writing and arithmetic; making it possible for children with numerous absences to catch up with the class; concrete aid with specific difficulties; personal attention to "problem children"; discovering weaknesses in children's problem-solving abilities which were helpful to the teacher; and making it possible for more children to have remedial help than would have been possible in any other way.[30]

Since retardation is a common problem of delinquents, school efforts to mitigate the difficulty would seem to be imperative. Harry Estill Moore has described this "retardation" not only in school work, but in total experiences, which leads to inadequate socialization in the culture as "conditioned participation." [31] By this he means that certain conditions within the social setting are limiting to the degree that developmental tasks, as Havighurst uses the term,[32] are not accomplished because of poverty of opportunity on one front or the other.

Notable among the many examples of special schools with special helps is the M. Gertrude Godvin School of Boston, Massachusetts. This school proudly reports [33] that, of 6000 boys over the past 20 years who were sent there because they had been pronounced unmanage-

[30] A progress report regarding "The Detroit School and Community Pilot Project for Reducing Juvenile Delinquency." First year. p. 16.

[31] Harry Estill Moore. "Definition of Conditioned Participation." *Dictionary of Sociology*, Henry Pratt Fairchild, editor. New York: Philosophical Society Library, 1944. p. 57.

[32] Robert J. Havighurst. *Human Development and Education*. New York: Longmans, Green and Company, 1953.

[33] Mary Handy. "Willingly—to School." *NEA Journal*, December 1955. p. 544-45.

able or had been truant again and again, 84 percent are living normal lives as responsible citizens. These boys, under the intelligent principalship of Agnes Lavery, are in a "disciplinary school" where their treatment is not "soft" and where they, with their parents, are taken before the juvenile judge for a court hearing if the enlightened rules of the school are repeatedly broken.[34]

Curriculum runs the gamut of needs at Godvin School, from classes in tailoring where boys make their own clothes, to preparation of "the best school lunches in Boston" where they learn to cook, to academic subjects where they are brought up to age-grade levels by special assistance in classes with boys of their own age and developmental stage. Because the relationship between school truancy and adult crime is exceedingly high—with one Massachusetts prison head estimating that 75 percent of the inmates of his prison had been truants—every effort is made to hold the interest of boys sent to Godvin through the adjusted curriculum and through the humane and warm approach to their problems.[35]

Still another example of an effective school program for handling the delinquent is the Philadelphia Case Review Committee which was organized to discover children with marked personality disorders.[36]

As Robert C. Taber writes, "In many classrooms in the country, there are human time bombs about to explode into criminal activity unless constructive steps are taken to prevent destructive blasts from taking place . . . ." [37]

In 1948, Louis P. Hoyer, superintendent of schools in Philadelphia, decided it would be wise to give help to youngsters with marked personality problems before they got into trouble. A school committee was formed of directors of the divisions of pupil personnel and counseling, medical services, special education, and the assistant to the board of superintendents, with Hoyer himself serving as chairman. This committee reviewed information from principals, teachers, attendance officers, counselors, school nurses, and psychologists concerning children and youth who appeared "potentially" dangerous in the classroom. Then the committee served as the connecting link between the home, the school, and the welfare agencies of Philadel-

[34] *Ibid.*, p. 545.
[35] *Ibid.*, p. 545.
[36] Robert C. Taber. "Before It's Too Late." *NEA Journal,* December 1953, p. 542-44.
[37] *Ibid.*, p. 542.

phia which have the resources to assist with problems uncovered by the case study committee. Success of this endeavor has come about because of the broad contacts which the school has with children; because the committee has been able to work swiftly and without red tape in getting help when help was needed, both for the child and his family; and finally, because of the breadth of information available to the committee, it could proceed with a therapeutic program involving the child, his family, and other situational factors involved in his difficulty. Taber concludes his description of this effort:

> Our schools can be a major factor in turning the tide of juvenile delinquency if we are willing to spend the time, effort, and money to organize a screening program and to provide the special services required to meet individual needs.[38]

Needless to say, examples of school programs effectively meeting problems of delinquents could be multiplied, but these that have been given may offer an indication of a variety of approaches which seem to have merit.

The Asocial Delinquent and the School

Teachers, Beck says, must give up their sentimental notions concerning "keeping children out of court" when they come up against the asocial delinquent. Youngsters devoid of conscience are dangerous whether they are victims of *anomie* or are "psychopathic personalities," or have "character disorders." From these youth come criminals who murder wantonly, who attack to maim and mutilate without reason or provocation, who seem to be without feelings as well as without conscience. Delay in dealing with them is a hazard, Beck reiterates, and "permissiveness only makes them worse." He feels these deviants should be brought to the attention of official agencies immediately before "tragic delinquency" occurs. The prognosis for them is not good. Beck makes it clear, these youth need a highly controlled environment or they need to be under institutional care for their own safety as well as for the protection of others. These delinquents, he believes, are in the main too damaged to be allowed to stay in school.[39]

Criticism has been leveled at William Jansen, superintendent of schools in New York City, for the over 900 youth suspended during February 1958. Many schoolteachers and administrators report it improved conditions in their schools "immeasurably." Others indicate

---

[38] *Ibid.*, p. 544.
[39] Beck, *op. cit.*, p. 63.

"society is only deferring the payment on its debt," as stated by Joseph C. Noethen, a district superintendent. He continues, "We are going to have to pay a high interest on it. Kicking the kids into the streets creates wolf packs. Suspension is supposed to have a therapuetic effect. Mass action destroys the therapeutic value."[40]

Robert M. MacIver, director of New York's Juvenile Delinquency Evaluation Project, notes that schools are the most stable social institutions many children ever encounter and it is the only one which can help them. "Bad as the adolescent may be in school," MacIver points out, "he is better behaved, a better member of society, in school than anywhere else."[41]

Beck, of course, does not imply that asocial delinquents or delinquents of any other character should be indiscriminately dumped from school because they create problems. However, he would insist that careful diagnosis, such as undertaken by the Philadelphia Case Review Committee, is advisable to discover the asocial delinquent and to protect youth and adult society alike from him.

The Neurotic Delinquent in School

Beck discusses neurotic delinquents and notes these develop in relatively rare instances and are small in number. Usually they come from upper and middle class families and have lacked warmth or acceptance in their family relations. A rigid and domineering father is sometimes responsible for the deviant behavior of his child. Delinquencies in this group include fire setting, sexual irregularities and crimes of violence. He points out that while teachers cannot cure neuroses, they can offer a relationship and opportunities for personal development that are beneficial to neurotic youth and which will help them function in an acceptable manner in spite of neuroses.[42]

Beck concludes that teachers working with delinquents of all types —and nondelinquents for that matter—need knowledge of child development; should have knowledge and skill in how to use themselves in constructive relationships with children and their parents; should be aware of their own personal needs in order to avoid obscuring the needs of children by their own. Moreover, he believes it imperative that teachers working with delinquents should have adequate salaries, working conditions which are satisfactory, an administrator who is

[40] Salisbury, *op. cit.,* p. 9.
[41] *Ibid.,* p. 9.
[42] Beck, *op. cit.,* p. 64.

intelligently supportive and understanding, and a flexible and adjustable curriculum geared to the youngsters. He advocates emphasis on developing teacher-potential as the first line of defense in working with delinquent youth in school rather than development of adjunctive services.[43]

The School and Prevention of Delinquency

To quote Robert MacIver again, the school is the only stable social organization which many delinquents know; the school is the only one which can help them.[44] From this it would appear that the more children and youth who do stay in school for more years, the greater will be the opportunity to assist even the delinquents toward responsible maturity as well as to contribute to the prevention of delinquent behavior. This, of course, must be within the limits of safety as pointed out by Beck.

Indicative of real improvement in school attendance is the recent *Biennial Survey of Education* reported in *School Life*, April 1957,[45] which revealed that for every 10 youngsters in the fifth grade in 1946-1947, the following schooling was completed: 9.2 out of each 10 finished the 8th grade; 8.7 out of 10 entered high school; 5.5 out of every 10 graduated from high school—a little over half; and finally 2.8 entered college.

Brownell points out that schools prevent delinquency when their aim is to educate all children by teaching each child according to his own abilities.[46] Schools with this approach find out what sort of person each child is and use this information intelligently. Schools, he believes, make up for lacks at home and in neighborhoods as has been indicated by others, and they should *strive to keep children in school*. Every child, he stresses, is an important human being and should be treated as such.

Four recommendations are offered by Brownell in prevention of delinquency through the school: (a) Each teacher must have a group of children to teach small enough so he can know and teach them as individuals. (b) Teachers need adequate preparation in how to work with children and youth and they must be interested in working with and helping them. (c) Special staffs should be available in

[43] *Ibid.*, p. 65.
[44] Salisbury, *op. cit.*, p. 9.
[45] *School Life*, April 1957, p. 13.
[46] Brownell, *op. cit.*, p. 53.

school systems to work with special problems and these specialists should include psychologists, school physicians, and social workers. (d) Finally, schools cannot accomplish their mission in delinquency prevention, Brownell believes, unless school programs and procedures are supported by parents and other community leaders. School programs, out of necessity, have to be designed to make possible adaptations for differences between fast and slow learners, between shy and aggressive children, and between groups vastly different in experiences, background and culture.

Delinquents, Brownell adds, are made, and not born. People have to come to understand needs of children and spend money to meet them. Schools, he stresses, share in the continuing educational process of home, school, and social institutions. His conclusion is that schools have to increase their effectiveness in doing their job if they carry their share of responsibility in delinquency prevention.[47]

It is indeed interesting to note that James B. Conant—former president of Harvard, former ambassador to West Germany, a chemist and long-time educator—arrives at almost the same conclusions concerning education in the public schools as does Brownell, though he approaches his discussion from the opposite pole, the problems of the gifted child.

Conant reports after a study of about 50 high schools "East, West, North and South."[48] He writes under the title, "Can Our High Schools Do the Job?" and Brownell might well have used a similar title in relation to the delinquent! To quote Conant:

> I am convinced that a satisfactory course of study for the bright boy or girl (the academically talented) can be offered in the public high school which is of a general or comprehensive type. . . . I am further convinced that the students in the comprehensive school derive certain advantages from their school years which are denied to their contemporaries in special schools.[49]

A good guidance system is "the keystone of the arch of public education," Conant points out, since it is here that aspirations, hopes, abilities and capacities can be determined and channeled into flexible groupings of areas of study to meet vast differences in young persons and their needs. One of the beauties of the comprehensive school, Dr. Conant states, is its flexibility so that "late bloomers" may be shifted from one course of study to another. In these schools, he notes, are opportunities for the intellectually gifted and for the average; for those who would pursue academic training to the peak of scientific

[47] *Ibid*, p. 64.
[48] Carnegie Corporation of New York. *Quarterly*, April 1958, p. 1-4.
[49] *Ibid.*, p. 2.

proficiency and for those who would complete their formal education at the end of high school; for those who will go into business and for those who will become skilled artisans in industry. In certain situations all of youth should share in common experiences, Conant believes, for the mutual benefit of each.[50]

Bertrand Russell once stated that the public schools of the United States were the single most powerful agent for "transforming a heterogeneous selection of mankind into a homogeneous nation."[51] This belief that the public schools can continue to serve basic democratic principles—the needs of all the children of all the people— Conant says, without slighting intellectual goals should "hearten a people who care about both the minds and the hearts of their children." [52] And it might well be added, a people who even care about their delinquents.

To achieve the aims of Brownell, no less than those of Conant, schools do have special needs. Garry Cleveland Myers points up a human aspect of the problem when he writes that research is needed on "how to establish wholesome restraint or how to balance restraint and love effectively—both at home and at school. Practically all of us agree on the value of love . . . But love without restraint seems to commit suicide while restraint without love also fails." [53]

Approaching this same problem of the schools and delinquency prevention from an entirely different point of view, F. V. Lehn, principal of the Waukegan Township Secondary Schools, asked his teachers to fill out a simple questionnaire concerning major problems of juvenile delinquency as they are directly related to the educational program of the school. His teachers listed the following:[54]

1. Parental indifference and lack of discipline in the home

2. Inadequate community recreational facilities and lack of motivation to participate in group activities

3. Too few high school courses designed for those not academically inclined, and in which slow learners may remain interested and succeed

4. Lack of teachers who have special training and who have the personality to deal successfully with delinquent students

5. Inadequate foster homes

6. Lack of training for young people before and after marriage as to

[50] *Ibid.*, p. 3.
[51] *Ibid.*, p. 4.
[52] *Ibid.*, p. 4.
[53] Letter, March 15, 1956.
[54] Letter, April 23, 1956.

their responsibilities, all of which would lead to a better home environment

7. The bad effect of behavior of delinquents and pre-delinquents on other student associates

8. The juvenile sophisticate who remains in school since he is not a delinquent though a disrupting influence

9. Indifference and neglect of spiritual obligations by parents, and the fact that delinquency flourishes even among church youth groups

10. Violations of the law by adults, which lead to lawlessness among children

11. Too free use of automobiles by students.

Note should be taken of the agreement of teachers in secondary schools with persons in research and school administration concerning delinquency and problems related to it. In fact, Beck stresses that the only hope of alleviation of the asocial delinquent and the neurotic is extensive education of young persons in high schools in child development, family living, and homemaking even as do the teachers of Waukegan in their Point 6.[55] Moreover, in their desire for flexibility in curriculum to meet the needs of slow learners and others with a variety of ambitions and aptitudes, they reflect the same point of view as that held by Brownell and Conant as well as other educational leaders.

Discussing this same problem of delinquency and the schools, Elizabeth Donovan, consultant, State Department of Education in Georgia, lists major areas for emphasis if the schools are to meet their responsibilities:

1. Better understanding of children, their characteristics, growth patterns, and development by teachers

2. Better communication between home and school

3. Improvement of diagnostic skills in determining problems in behavior and their severity

4. Better and closer working relationships between schools and community agencies concerned with programs for children and youth

5. Broader curriculum offerings to meet individual interests and needs

6. Pulling together information on ways of helping boys and girls develop their own basic values

7. Assumption of responsibility by the schools, churches and other community groups in getting juvenile courts established in counties where they do not exist and in providing desirable detention centers for children and youth who must be held in custody.[56]

[55] Beck, *op. cit.*, p. 64.
[56] Letter, March 12, 1956.

These presentations by educators working in the schools of the United States state in slightly different terms what William C. Kvaraceus has written of delinquency and the schools in an article, "Preventing and Treating Juvenile Delinquency—Some Basic Approaches," [57] and in his book, *The Community and the Delinquent.*[58] Kvaraceus, in his article, writes that it is becoming possible to spot delinquency earlier and that referral to proper sources of treatment and help is a major contribution in prevention. As a close second to this premise, he insists, as did Beck, Brownell, Robert L. Sutherland and Donovan, that child study is an essential for teachers if they are to perform their diagnostic functions successfully and are to assist with individualized planning for treatment of youngsters with special problems. He is convinced that no hope exists for the delinquent unless guidance personnel, psychologists, psychiatrists and psychiatric social workers are easily accessible to the individual child through the school and the community. Treatment, Kvaraceus stresses, must be specifically designed to meet *personal, social* and *environmental* needs of the deviant child—and he calls this the community aspect of child study.

Corollaries to the above basic principles, Kvaraceus lists as coordination of all community resources for children, money to develop intensive child study and diagnostic programs in schools, and the establishment of programs of diagnosis and treatment, both by school and community as a whole, on the basis of proven knowledge which is the reflection of scientific research.[59]

Continuing Education and Delinquency

Harrison Salisbury, in his description of home and community situations out of which delinquency grows, discusses the inadequate preparation of parents for homemaking and child rearing.[60] He states that thousands of families were moved into housing projects in New York City without preparation for living in these new kinds of quarters. Moreover, the families who were in the neighborhood before the advent of the newcomers were ill prepared to receive and live with the families moving into public housing.

[57] William C. Kvaraceus. "Preventing and Treating Juvenile Delinquency— Some Basic Approaches." *The School Review,* December 1955. p. 477-79.

[58] William C. Kvaraceus. *The Community and the Delinquent.* New York: World Book Company, 1954.

[59] William C. Kvaraceus. "Preventing and Treating Juvenile Delinquency— Some Basic Approaches." *op. cit.,* p. 478-79.

[60] Salisbury, *op. cit.,* p. 6-7.

The Dallas Public Schools in cooperation with the Dallas Housing Authority and the Home and Family Life Division, Texas State Department of Education, have met these two problems by an intensive homemaking education program for adults with many of the centers for education in the housing projects themselves. At these study centers, home economics teachers have developed everything from rudimentary instruction in housekeeping and cleanliness, through child care and development, to basic nutrition and cooking, sewing and care of clothing, to family and community interpersonal relations. Work has been done with family groups, on their own problems as well as with groups of homemakers. This program has been in operation for nearly 12 years under the direction of Mrs. Ona Redmon, with 10 or more teachers of adults on her staff. This is one excellent example of the coordination of community resources through school leadership in its home and family life education division.

Kvaraceus stresses the necessity of bridging the gap between home and school in prevention of delinquency, and he indicates parent education is of paramount importance. "Parent education" involves not only study of behavior of children but of the total processes of homemaking and family living. Moreover, parent education of necessity includes actual participation of parents in the learning processes rather than simply listening to "guest speakers." [61]

Robert L. Sutherland writes of education for home living and parenthood:

The first specialist to stress mental health in many schools was the person once called the "parent educator," who now bears the more modern and complicated title of "teacher of adults in home and family life education." This teacher, employed by the public schools, devotes his or her full time in organizing discussion groups with parents and, through other educational methods, helping parents join with teachers in basing their work with children upon scientific knowledge of the processes of human growth and development. [62]

Summary

Little doubt exists, then, that the schools have multiple roles to play in prevention of delinquency and in handling delinquents among their in-school population. Kvaraceus' listing of the important areas of school

[61] William C. Kvaraceus. *The Community and the Delinquent*. p. 252-59.

[62] Robert L. Sutherland. "Delinquency and Mental Health." *Federal Probation*, March 1957. Reprint, Austin, Texas: The Hogg Foundation for Mental Health, The University of Texas. (Page numbers refer to the reprint.) p. 4.

life which contribute to the prevention and control of delinquency will serve as a summary:

School superintendents function in delinquency prevention and control in two capacities—in stimulating the interrelationship between the school and the community and in the overall improvement of the school setting and program for the education of *all* children—deviant and normal alike.

Schools, themselves, through teachers, special school services personnel, and administrators have to develop competence in evaluating the effectiveness of the school program in terms of controlling undesirable behavior as well as in terms of grades and promotions.

Every effort has to be made to select better trained school personnel on all levels from the school custodian through teachers to the top administrator, who know how to work with children and youth and who are interested in working with them.

Child study by teachers should be a continuing part of their inservice education toward effective diagnosis of behavior problems and for referral either to specialized services within the school or to community agencies designed for such treatment and care.

An effective guidance program—as Conant stressed—is an imperative for prevention and control of delinquency as it is for the maximum in opportunity for the "gifted" and the average child.

More extensive use of the case conference is indicated for study and treatment of individual children with problems—as demonstrated by the Philadelphia Case Study Committee.

Improving flexible curriculum offerings and teaching methods for all youth is essential, but it is especially necessary in order to maintain interest and offer satisfaction to youth of limited experiences and background in home and neighborhood.

Policies of promotion, grading, discipline, and handling truancy need to be upgraded to prevent development of intense feelings of defeat and inferiority with hostility toward the schools on the part of youngsters whose basic experiences in themselves imply limitation of success in school.

Continuing and expanding cooperation with the home is imperative through the use of school social workers, through welcoming parents to the school for conferences and participation, and through home and family life education programs for parents developed by the schools.

Finally, the school has major responsibility in interpreting the role of schools in delinquency prevention and control to both boards of education and to the communities as wholes stressing the need for funds to enrich the total school program as well as to make possible special flexibility of curriculum and services for children and youth with special needs.[63]

[63] Based on and paraphrased from Kvaraceus, "The Central Role of the Schools," *The Community and the Delinquent*, Chapter 10, p. 265-317. See also: William C. Kvaraceus, *Delinquent Behavior*, Vols. 1 and 2, Washington, D. C.: National Education Association, 1959.